P9-AFD-471

HOW TO GET
THE RAISE YOU WANT IN
90 DAYS OR LESS:

A Step-by-Step Plan
for Making It Happen

by Kathy M. Barnes-Hemsworth

Library Resource Center
Renton Technical College
3000 N.E. 4th Street
Renton, WA 98056

HOW TO GET THE RAISE YOU WANT IN 90 DAYS OR LESS: A STEP-BY-STEP PLAN FOR MAKING IT HAPPEN

Copyright© 2010 Atlantic Publishing Group, Inc.
1405 SW 6th Avenue • Ocala, Florida 34471 • Phone 800-814-1132 • Fax 352-622-1875

Web site: www.atlantic-pub.com • E-mail: sales@atlantic-pub.com
SAN Number: 268-1250

No part of this publication may be reproduced, stored in a retrieval system, or transmitted in any form or by any means, electronic, mechanical, photocopying, recording, scanning, or otherwise, except as permitted under Section 107 or 108 of the 1976 United States Copyright Act, without the prior written permission of the Publisher. Requests to the Publisher for permission should be sent to Atlantic Publishing Group, Inc., 1405 SW 6th Avenue, Ocala, Florida 34471.

ISBN 13: 9781601382863   ISBN 10: 1-60138-286-3

Library of Congress Cataloging-in-Publication Data

Barnes, Kathy, 1972-
  How to get the raise you want in 90 days or less : a step-by-step plan for making it happen / by Kathy Barnes.
     p. cm.
  Includes bibliographical references and index
  ISBN-13: 978-1-60138-286-3 (alk. paper)
  ISBN-10: 1-60138-286-3 (alk. paper)
  1. Promotions. 2. Wages. I. Title.
  HF5549.5.P7B366 2009
  650.14--dc22
                          2008038305

650.14 BARNES 2010

Barnes, Kathy, 1972-

How to get the raise you want in 90 days or less

LIMIT OF LIABILITY/DISCLAIMER OF WARRANTY: The publisher and the author make no representations or warranties with respect to the accuracy or completeness of the contents of this work and specifically disclaim all warranties, including without limitation warranties of fitness for a particular purpose. No warranty may be created or extended by sales or promotional materials. The advice and strategies contained herein may not be suitable for every situation. This work is sold with the understanding that the publisher is not engaged in rendering legal, accounting, or other professional services. If professional assistance is required, the services of a competent professional should be sought. Neither the publisher nor the author shall be liable for damages arising herefrom. The fact that an organization or Web site is referred to in this work as a citation and/or a potential source of further information does not mean that the author or the publisher endorses the information the organization or Web site may provide or recommendations it may make. Further, readers should be aware that Internet Web sites listed in this work may have changed or disappeared between when this work was written and when it is read.

Printed in the United States

PROJECT MANAGER: Amanda Miller • amiller@atlantic-pub.com
INTERIOR DESIGN: T.L. Price • design@tlpricefreelance.com
PEER REVIEWER: Marilee Griffin • mgriffin@atlantic-pub.com
ASSISTANT EDITOR: Angela Pham • apham@atlantic-pub.com
FRONT AND BACK COVER DESIGN: Jackie Miller • millerjackiej@gmail.com

Printed on Recycled Paper

We recently lost our beloved pet "Bear," who was not only our best and dearest friend but also the "Vice President of Sunshine" here at Atlantic Publishing. He did not receive a salary but worked tirelessly 24 hours a day to please his parents. Bear was a rescue dog that turned around and showered myself, my wife, Sherri, his grandparents

Jean, Bob, and Nancy, and every person and animal he met (maybe not rabbits) with friendship and love. He made a lot of people smile every day.

We wanted you to know that a portion of the profits of this book will be donated to The Humane Society of the United States. *–Douglas & Sherri Brown*

The human-animal bond is as old as human history. We cherish our animal companions for their unconditional affection and acceptance. We feel a thrill when we glimpse wild creatures in their natural habitat or in our own backyard.

Unfortunately, the human-animal bond has at times been weakened. Humans have exploited some animal species to the point of extinction.

The Humane Society of the United States makes a difference in the lives of animals here at home and worldwide. The HSUS is dedicated to creating a world where our relationship with animals is guided by compassion. We seek a truly humane society in which animals are respected for their intrinsic value, and where the human-animal bond is strong.

Want to help animals? We have plenty of suggestions. Adopt a pet from a local shelter, join The Humane Society and be a part of our work to help companion animals and wildlife. You will be funding our educational, legislative, investigative and outreach projects in the U.S. and across the globe.

Or perhaps you'd like to make a memorial donation in honor of a pet, friend or relative? You can through our Kindred Spirits program. And if you'd like to contribute in a more structured way, our Planned Giving Office has suggestions about estate planning, annuities, and even gifts of stock that avoid capital gains taxes.

Maybe you have land that you would like to preserve as a lasting habitat for wildlife. Our Wildlife Land Trust can help you. Perhaps the land you want to share is a backyard— that's enough. Our Urban Wildlife Sanctuary Program will show you how to create a habitat for your wild neighbors.

So you see, it's easy to help animals. And The HSUS is here to help.

2100 L Street NW • Washington, DC 20037 • 202-452-1100
www.hsus.org

Author Dedication

This book is dedicated to my husband, Shawn, and our daughter, Elizabeth, as well as my parents, Billy and Charlcie Barnes. In addition, it is dedicated to three wonderful friends: Claire Crouch, Jane Myers, and Tammy Smith. I would also like to thank everyone who participated in the case studies.

Table of Contents

Chapter 10: Tailor Yourself to Meet Their Needs 179

Chapter 11: Prepare and Assemble Your Case 189

PART III: Taking Your Case to Your Boss 215

Chapter 12: Take Your Case to the Boss 217

Foreword

by Robyn Feldberg, CCMC, NCRW

I n *How to Get the Raise You Want in 90 Days or Less: A Step-by-Step Plan for Making It Happen*, author Kathy M. Barnes-Hemsworth has succeeded in creating a comprehensive go-to resource for people serious about turning their financial goals into a reality and implementing a plan to heighten and earn their value in today's competitive employment market.

With every fiber of my being, I believe that it is every person's inalienable right to create a career that allows them to earn an abundant salary, still have a personal life, enjoy what they do, and feel successful, happy, and healthy. The skills that it takes to create this type of career, however, are not innate to us, but rather

Library Resource Center
Renton Technical College
3000 N.E. 4th Street
Renton, WA 98056

something that most of us need to learn, and Kathy's book is a smart and sensible place to acquire the necessary knowledge one needs to build a stable career foundation.

Though the money one earns from his or her career does not dictate the level of their personal fulfillment or satisfaction, it certainly does help pay the bills and make life more comfortable. What keeps most people from creating the career of their dreams from a financial perspective is not a lack of ability, a lack of hard work, or a lack of education — it is a lack of planning and intention. Like the old adage goes, "He who fails to plan, plans to fail."

As companies get leaner and budgets continue to get tighter, employees have to become smarter, more strategic, more competent, and more confident than ever before; they must learn to communicate a strong brand in the workplace and a unique promise of value. Just as cream always rises to the top, employees with strong brands who are perceived as delivering greater value will always be in demand and able to command higher wages — even in economic downturns.

As a certified career management coach, one of my greatest joys is found in equipping my clients with the mechanics and mindset necessary to support their career development. In my professional life, there is nothing more rewarding than helping my client's transition from stuck to unstuck, from victim to victorious, and from under-earning to financially successful. To this end, I am constantly looking for new resources that I can recommend, and I recommend this book to anyone seeking solid, reliable information on how to get a raise.

Library Resource Center
Renton Technical College
3000 N.E. 4th Street
Renton, WA 98056

Congratulations to you for picking up this book and taking steps to intentionally steer your career where you want it to go. Obviously, you already recognize how critical it is for you to ask for what you want and have a realistic, cohesive, and actionable plan in place that will allow you to safely reach your goals in the fastest and most efficient manner possible. I wish you all the best as you start reading this book and begin your journey toward a place of greater abundance and prosperity.

In support of your Abundant Success,
Robyn Feldberg, CCMC, NCRW
"The Abundant Success Career Coach"
Owner, Abundant Success Career Services
www.AbundantSuccessCareerServices.com
(972) 464-1144

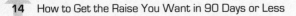

Robyn Feldberg, "The Abundant Success Career Coach" and owner of Abundant Success Career Services, has established herself as a recognized leader in the careers industry. With more than 17 years' experience and credentials as a Certified Career Management Coach (CCMC) and one of only three Nationally Certified Résumé Writers (NCRW) in Texas, Robyn has equipped hundreds of professionals with the tools, techniques, and motivation to create careers that are personally, professionally, and financially fulfilling. In addition to five published contributions to national career books, Robyn has been featured numerous times on the award-winning ABC television talk show Good Morning Texas, *interviewed and quoted by **www. Monster.com** and* The Washington Business Journal, *and is currently serving as the president of the National Résumé Writers' Association. For more information about Robyn or her business, please visit her Web site at **www.AbundantSuccessCareerServices.com** or call her at (972) 464-1144.*

Introduction

This book is organized into three parts:

1. Understanding Business Basics
2. Getting Ready for Your Raise
3. Taking Your Case to Your Boss

These sections have been selected to allow you to make a natural progression through the material and become the perfect candidate to secure your pay raise. You will be much better suited to make preparations to pursue your raise after you understand how business structure works and where you fit in that structure.

Likewise, you will have a much stronger case to present to your boss if you fully prepare to pursue a pay raise.

Your employer may feel he or she risks quite a bit by giving you a paycheck at all, let alone giving more money than you are currently making. The organization of this book will take you through a natural understanding of how to help your business see your value and reward you with the raise you deserve.

Each part is broken into a number of universal steps to complete before moving on to the next phase of preparation to request your pay raise. The steps include:

- **Employee evaluations.** In this section, you will learn to see yourself as your employer sees you.

- **Mastering the basics.** This section will be a primer in helping you reach your potential and become the best employee possible.

- **Brand yourself.** Here you will learn how to make yourself stand out from the rest of the employees in your office.

- **Tailor yourself to meet their needs.** It is not enough to be a good employee; you will also need to be the kind of employee that your company wants to promote. This section will walk you through how to become that employee.

- **Preparing and assembling your case.** By this point, you will have done a considerable amount of work. Now you will have to put it together in a coherent way that your boss will appreciate and understand.

- **Prepare and assemble your case.** All your work is useless if you do not conduct a good meeting with your boss. This section explains, in detail, how to explain to your boss that you are ready for a pay raise, and why you deserve one.

Each of these steps is broken into several individual tasks that are fully explained, with lists and comments from experts to easily guide you through this process.

Obviously, the publishers of this book cannot guarantee that your boss is a reasonable person who will respond favorably to your request. What we can tell you, though, is that after reading this book and following these steps, you will be a fantastic candidate for a raise.

PART I
Understanding Business Basics

Now that you have decided to pursue your career goals and get the raise that you deserve — or will soon deserve — it is important to start at the beginning. This first section will help you look at the nuts and bolts of business, and how you can use those tools to begin building your case.

CHAPTER 1

Understanding How Business Works, and How You Work into Business

Before you ask for a raise, it is crucial to understand basic business structure. This will allow you to better assess your company's goals and priorities and tailor your raise pitch to meet their needs. Also, understanding how employee compensation is calculated, why companies are reluctant to give someone more money, and why you should even ask them for a raise will give you the confidence you need to make a strong case that your employer simply cannot ignore.

Profit, Non-Profit, and Government Agencies

Business structures are dependent upon the type of organization, whether it is a for-profit, non-profit, or government agency.

Basic Business Structures

The purpose of non-profit agencies is to provide services and/or benefits to the general public. Any profits raised by the agency are considered surplus and are used to help provide future services and programs to clients.

For-profit businesses are just that — businesses designed to earn money for shareholders and investors.

Government agencies can be on the local level, such as city or county, or may branch out into larger organizations, such as those run by the state or federal government.

How Employee Compensation is Calculated

Employers can pay their employees with one of two methods. Compensation can either be given in "wages" or "salaries." A wage is based on how many hours an employee works, while a salary is the amount paid for a job to get done, regardless of hours worked. Both terms mean employees are getting paid; they just have slightly different connotations and conditions.

Salaries tend to be given to executives and administrative and professional employees, while wages are most often given to more labor-intensive positions, like store clerks or maintenance workers. Salaries tend to show up as a certain amount of money on a paycheck each week, without a specific counting of hours. Waged employees tend to have to fill out specific time cards, and each hour is calculated into the pay. Regardless of whether you are given wages or a salary, you are within your rights to ask for a raise. The steps included in this book will apply to either type of position.

The Fair Labors and Standards Act (FLSA) regulates setting wages or salaries for employees. The Act was established in 1938 but is regularly revised. Among other things, it provides minimum standards for both wages and overtime entitlement and spells out administrative procedures by which covered work time must be compensated. On July 24, 2009, the federally set minimum wage increased to $7.25 per hour.

With the creation of minimum wage through the FLSA in 1938, employers in every state were required to pay their workers at least a certain amount set by the government. Each year, officials review the current minimum wage, and revisions are made to keep minimum wage a livable wage. There is debate as to whether workers can survive on minimum wage, but this is the lowest amount employers can start considering when employee compensation is determined.

After getting the basics of the law down, employers examine many aspects to decide how much to pay for a job, and then, more specifically, how much to pay for each employee.

Supply and demand

Supply and demand is the most basic of economic concepts. Supply refers to how much of a commodity there is in a market, and demand refers to how many people want that commodity. In terms of employees, the commodity is the person and his or her work.

When an employer is looking to fill a relatively low-skilled position, they will find that there are many people who could do that job. Jobs like maintenance work or simple retail sales do not require a fine-tuned skill level; essentially, any employee can be trained to do these things. This is not a judgment on the worker or the work; it is simply a reflection of the job's difficulty level. Because there is such a vast number of people available to do this work, employers do not feel pressure to pay more. If one employee is not happy with the wages offered, the employer will not likely have difficulty finding another worker to fill that position.

High-skilled occupations will demand higher compensation. It is more difficult to find an incredibly skilled marketer or salesperson who can close a sale with any customer. Executives and high-end assistants are more difficult to come by because they are in lower supply, so companies tend to be willing to pay more for them.

Job title, description, and overall duties

Ideally, the more work and responsibility a job requires, the more the employee performing those duties will get paid. If the job is relatively simple, without too many tasks assigned to it, employers generally will not feel pressured to pay a higher wage because not as much work will be getting done.

Likewise, if there are many tiers to a position, the employees in the higher tiers will typically be paid more. For example, if one account executive handles three accounts, and another handles seven accounts, the executive who handles more accounts and thus more responsibilities will likely receive more pay.

There is also a hierarchy inherent in titles:

- Assistant
- Coordinator
- Manager
- Executive
- Vice president

There is a linear progression to the preceding terms. Inherent in each successive title is generally increased workload, stress, responsibility, and return to the company. Therefore, as an employee progresses through each title, the amount of his or her paychecks will increase accordingly.

When employers set salaries, they also try to make them competitive in relation to the work performed. Using this method, employers attract the best talent for the job. If an employer sets their salaries too low, talented potential employees will not want to work for them, assuming they would be able to make more elsewhere.

What a job adds to the company

The truth is that every job adds considerably to a company. Though the title of janitor or custodian may not be a glamorous position, it is crucial that the office be kept clean. A senior account executive would have a hard time concentrating on developing creative new marketing strategies if her office is saturated with week-old garbage. Likewise, the mailroom employees may not need to have a higher-level degree to complete their daily duties, but the company could not function if there were not a system in place to deliver and receive correspondence.

Nevertheless, the aspect that a typical company is inevitably most concerned with is acquiring money for itself. If a job directly affects how much money a company makes, the employee in that position will be paid a higher amount. It may be true that at the end of the day, a janitor makes it possible for a company to earn more money. However, an account executive gets someone to write checks to the company, for example, and consequently, that particular employee is rewarded with a larger paycheck. The more clearly a company can see how a particular employee's job creates more money for the company, the more likely it is that that employee will be paid a greater amount.

How the job has changed over time

Because of technological advances, the executive assistant job you applied for two years ago is much different today than it was then. There are new electronic ways of scheduling meetings and arranging flights; sending memos now involves some desktop publishing knowledge; and intranets have changed the way supplies are ordered. The knowledge required to do the job is more sophisticated and, therefore, commands a higher pay rate.

In addition to the changes from technological advances, positions inside a company tend to evolve over time. A position may become more inclusive and demand a higher salary than it did a year ago. The U.S. economy relies on the increasing talent of its workforce to set higher wages. Employers want to see their workers come in with a higher level of skill sophistication, and those who have those skills get paid higher wages.

Unfortunately for many workers, this trend toward workers with cutting-edge skills undeniably favors the younger end of the workforce, as technology is now automatically built into their schooling and their day-to-day life. Consumer technology is currently being marketed toward younger generations. Computer and cell phone companies want this young demographic to boost their sales, so the younger generations are integrally exposed to the newest in gadgets and technological advances. This is in contrast to employees in their 40s who may have to go back to school and take classes to thoroughly understand computer programming or Internet research.

The point is that new technology is out there, and it is constantly changing. Companies tend to be willing to pay more for an employee who can keep up with technological advances. Employees who do not understand technology, or who do not make an effort to keep their technology skills current, are more likely to see smaller paychecks — unless they take the initiative to improve their skills and become informed of the latest technological advances.

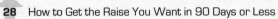

CHAPTER

Finances

_____

The State of the Economy

Recessions and downturns in the economy affect us all. When times are tough, customers do not spend as much money; when customers are not spending as much money, businesses are not making as much money. And when businesses are not making as much, employees do not get paid as much. If an employee starts working at a company during a slow economic period, that company may not be willing to give their new employee as much money; the company may even ask new employees to share the burden by taking less pay or working fewer hours to cut costs even further.

Inversely, if the economy is booming when a company hires a new employee, the company may be more willing to pay the employee a higher rate of pay. During good times, businesses are free to share their wealth, and sharing their wealth makes for happier employees who will, in return, work harder, which results in making more money for the business. When a company has money to spare, it will likely pass along the good fortune to all involved customers, who may see a decrease in prices or an increase in quality. New employees may see higher starting salaries or wages.

Cost of Living

You may find that an executive in New York City makes a greater salary than an executive for the same business living in Topeka, Kansas. The cost of living varies from city to city and affects how much employers in various cities pay their employees. Companies in expensive cities — like Los Angeles, New York City, Chicago, or San Francisco — usually need to pay their employees more in order to retain them and prevent high employee turnover.

The cost of living is typically more expensive in large metropolitan settings. Skilled employees will not let their skills be used at a rate that does not support their lifestyle; strong workers will jump ship when they find a company willing to pay them more. It is not just greed on the part of workers. Instead, it is about workers needing to pay their rent in cities where it costs more for basic living expenses. By the same token, companies in less expensive cities will not have to pay their employees as much because the cost of living is not as high.

Non-Salary Benefits

In addition to money in a paycheck, employees can also be paid with a variety of benefits. The law does not require companies to give their employees benefits in addition to the percentages companies have to pay, such as unemployment insurance, social security, and workers' compensation. However, because of mutual advantages for the employee as well as the employer, many organizations offer some kind of benefits package.

If an employee has a strong benefits package, there may be some money held from their paycheck, which actually aids both the employer and the employee: The employee gets other expenses paid, while the company has extra funds to invest in itself.

Although the preceding information seems to suggest that the best way you can ensure a large paycheck is to be fortunate enough to land a higher-skilled job during a booming economic period, workers cannot choose what jobs are available during their job search. Regardless of when you got your job or how much you are getting paid now, understanding how salaries are set will help you negotiate your new salary.

You should also understand that despite all the factors that go into determining an employee's pay rate, employers have plenty of incentive to pay their employees much more than the minimum requirement. Paying employees well provides many advantages to a company, including increased employee loyalty, lower staff turnover, and happier workplaces.

Problems with Giving Someone a Raise

Though companies like to reward their employees when possible, there are some problems inherent in giving someone a pay raise. Nothing is free, and rewarding you may cause issues elsewhere for the company. Your employer will definitely weigh any potential problems against giving a pay raise.

The biggest problem for a company when it comes to giving any employee more money is that it also means less money for someone or something else in the company. Money used for a pay raise has to come from somewhere in the coffers, such as from the profits, the savings, or the investments. You may think a few hundred extra dollars is no big deal to a giant company, but to any company, dollars are king. Losing money, for whatever reason, is not good business.

Often, a raise will come with extra duties or even a job promotion. If that happens, your old duties now need to be done by someone else, as the company now has to re-figure how they rank positions and people. This is not efficient and may lead to the loss of more dollars, as employees are temporarily less productive when positions are being moved around.

In the next chapter, we will look at the employee review process and see how employers begin to determine whether an employee is deserving of a raise, if he or she asks for one.

Employee Evaluations

Companies tend to give their employees some sort of regular performance evaluation. These are not mandated by law, but performance evaluations protect both the company and the employee from misunderstandings that can become problems later.

The strongest employees will use the review process to their advantage. Reviews are a time to tout your achievements and discuss the positive work that you have done. If your employer tells you something that you disagree with or do not understand, be sure to ask him or her for clarification.

Employee Reviews: How They Work for You and for Them

Just because something is good for you does not mean it necessarily *feels* good — and that holds true for employee reviews. They can serve as useful tools, but both employers and employees can be leery of annual performance reviews, whether the review happens through a sit-down meeting, or by a memo sheet detailing what the employee is doing right and wrong.

For employers, there is often a considerable amount of paperwork and sometimes seemingly arbitrary criteria on which to grade their subordinates. Plus, it takes time to sit down with someone and review, in detail, all the compiled information. The average review-giver does not relish the chance to tell employees what they are doing wrong, and there is always the risk of arguments or tension in the office after reports are given and concrete grades have been distributed.

For the employees, there is that cold feeling in the pit of their stomach as they have to listen to a list of their boss's grievances with them. There may be items on their review that they did not even know were there, and they may feel defensive as they listen to someone grade them out loud. Employees may even be left to wonder whether the review is an honest assessment of their skills and shortcomings — or just a chance for an employer to take out his or her bad day on you.

The review process can be a good tool for moving ahead in business. There is value to the employer and the employee when standards and expectations are outlined, explained, and evaluated. Research shows that more than 80 percent of employers and employees normally favor some sort of review process to make sure everyone is on the same page. With a clear review system in place, employees ideally will be more efficient, feel happier with their place at work, and feel more loyal to their companies. They can easily make performance reviews work to their benefit. A review is not only the perfect chance to find out how you are doing, but to remind your employers of work you have done that is worthy of a pay raise. The review should not simply be a time when an employee sits quietly and listens. Prepared employees can use this time proactively to market themselves to their employers as someone who is doing well and who deserves improved pay or benefits for their work performance.

Performance reviews were developed to help employers manage their employees, and to also protect companies from the complaints of disgruntled workers. In the last 20 or 30 years, employee reviews have become fairly standard practice.

The fact that employee reviews are often performed, but not regulated, means companies differ greatly as to how and when they give reviews. Some companies emphasize individual work, while others focus on how well the employee works in groups.

Furthermore, some companies allow the worker to fill out his or her own review to discuss with the supervisor, while others leave all the evaluation to the supervisor. Whatever the method, the objective is to keep employees and employers in agreement about duties, expectations, and concerns — and to address problems before they become too serious.

To learn more about your employer's policy on giving employee reviews, speak with the human resources department. If you believe it is time for you to get a pay raise, schedule an appointment for a review, and make sure it happens. This would be in your best interest, especially if you are trying to earn a pay raise. You will not be able to know where you need to be to get a raise without a clear discussion with your employer.

Negative feedback

Ideally, your review will go well. You want to get glowing reviews, and frankly, your employer most likely wants to give you a good report as well. After all, a good review means that everything is fine at worst, and fantastic at best. However, many issues can contribute to bad marks on an employee's review. These can include:

- Poor performance
- Lack of enthusiasm for work
- Regular tardiness
- Excessive personal Internet or phone use
- Unexplained or excessive absences
- Lack of involvement in company activities

If you do receive negative feedback on a review, it is crucial to fully understand the issue so you can correct it as quickly as possible. The faster you understand the problem, the more efficiently you can make corrections. You should ask exactly what the problem is and what steps the employer would like to see followed in order to correct the problem. Do not assume you know how to fix the problem. Check with your employer to make sure you are getting yourself back on the right track.

It is possible that negative feedback may be the result of a misunderstanding. Perhaps you were unaware of one of your boss's expectations, or there may be issues your employer does not know about that would change his or her opinion of your performance — for example, if you have been picking up the slack for another employee who is absent or negligent in his or her duties, which may affect the performance of your own work. If something like this is the case, it is imperative for you to discuss this during your meeting so your employer can re-evaluate your performance.

Preparing for your review

Regardless of how often your company gives reviews or what method it uses to give them, you will want to make sure you get the most out of your review. It is a necessary part of business life and can be the first step on your way toward getting the raise you want and deserve. It can be a nerve-wracking experience, but some basic tips can help you have a positive employee review.

- Before your review appointment, ask what will be covered so you know what will be discussed and can prepare any questions.

- Collect evidence of your work, including positive e-mails, notes, or memos from supervisors or clients; awards; or official recognition. These items can be helpful in soliciting positive conversation from your reviewer.

- Get any feedback in advance. Set up an informal meeting with your employer so you can reduce negative feedback on the formal, written review.

- Prepare a list of goals. Let your reviewer know you are looking to move into a higher-ranking position than you hold currently.

- Maintain eye contact, smile, and ask questions. Listening actively will help you understand, and not just hear, what your employer is telling you. Ask questions if you do not understand something.

- Remember to relax, because these reviews are just as stressful for your boss as they are for you. Take a deep breath so you can calm yourself before your meeting, smile, and be polite and personable throughout the entire meeting.

According to Peter Villanova, a professor at Appalachian State University, while there are no laws per se governing performance reviews, there are union agreements, and there are procedures prescribed within each organization that regulate how, when, and by whom performance reviews are conducted. There is considerable latitude and variety in performance reviews. The Supreme Court, for example, has on numerous occasions reviewed cases involving performance reviews, but it only does so to adjudicate as to whether existing law or constitutional mandates have been fulfilled. It does not wish to establish prescriptions for good business practice — that is the duty of the business organization.

Questions on performance reviews take the form of accounts for how a goal was achieved or not achieved, what could have made it achievable, what support was essential to meeting the goal, or what support was needed, but absent. Also, questions are future-oriented, such as what goals are feasible and what would be required to meet the goal in the way of organizational support.

In some organizations, the process ends when the performance review is completed and the review is filed away in a database. In others, it is used as a basis of judgment for the next annual review. It may be subject to approval by a second-level supervisor in some organizations. Most often, when all signatures have been obtained and the feedback session completed, the review is filed away.

Often, the interview is when any changes may occur to the review itself. Changes subsequent to those are a reflection of a successful appeal. The best way for the employee to get a change in the review is from his or her supervisor. The interview is the occasion to provide information and to persuade the evaluator that a change is warranted. Any other occasion, such as the time following the interview, would require a challenge to the record, which could open potential conflict with the evaluator. The most effective appeal for a change has information to support the request and is delivered in a non-threatening manner.

In some circumstances, an employee may request a review. Most likely, though, the employee is evaluated on the anniversary date of hire or at the end of a probationary period.

Benefits accrue to the employee and the organization when performance reviews are conducted responsibly. Employees can more accurately gauge their effectiveness and their competence, giving feedback about further career advancement prospects and value to the firm. Organizations are provided with diagnostic information, which provides better assessment of their success or allows them to identify weaknesses in the execution of their business plan.

During a review, employees should avoid broadcasting a sense of detachment to the review. If the supervisor is held accountable for doing the review, and the process allows a way the organization could use the review data for meaningful personnel decisions, the employee's appearing that he or she is above the review will only frustrate the supervisor and make it likely that the supervisor will invest less energy in the employee's future success with the organization.

CASE STUDY: MICHELE PURYEAR HERNDON

Michele Puryear Herndon
Quality assurance manager
Newport, Tennessee

Michele Puryear Herndon, a quality assurance manager at a company that manufactures automotive-related machinery in Newport, Tennessee, points out that an employee needs to make an appointment to meet with the supervisor to request a pay raise. "Don't catch me off-guard and without notice," she said. "Make an appointment to see me."

Herndon said the employee needs to show financial reasons to justify a raise, such as showing why you deserve a raise "for doing what you were paid to do in the past." As an example, Herndon said she introduced and helped implement a plan that decreased scrap within the company by $4,000 in May 2009.

She also expects an employee to show continuous support, she said. "Show me ideas of other ways for improvement within the company without putting down co-workers."

Herndon said an employee should work for the company at least six months before asking for a raise, and the employee should be going above the current job requirements. "Show me that you are stepping up and trying to do the next-level job (where appropriate)."

Why 90 Days?

There may be books that promise a raise in a week, or more money by your next lunch meeting, but those sort of promises are not realistic. Maybe you are a super employee, ready and deserving of demanding more from your boss; even so, there is much to do to prepare to lobby successfully for your raise. It is not impossible work, but it *is* work, and you need to make sure you are ready to do it.

Asking for a raise prematurely and without the proper preparation will not only hurt your chances for a raise right now, but it may also impair your chances for getting a raise in the future. If you go in unprepared, your boss will notice, and you will have an uphill battle to change those perceptions later.

It will take time to become the type of employee who can successfully lobby for a raise at all; it will take time to prove to your employers — and yourself — that you are committed to the kind of work it takes to earn more money in your paycheck each week. There is also a considerable amount of research and preparation involved.

Just like an attorney takes weeks, months, or sometimes years to prepare the best case for his or her client, it will take time to prepare the best case possible to show your boss that you are serious about what you are asking for — and that you deserve every penny.

Nevertheless, the steps in this book will successfully guide you through what it takes to demonstrate that you deserve the raise you are pursuing. Nothing says you will not get through the work before the 90 days have passed; if you manage to do so, go for it. Three months, though, is a perfectly reasonable time in which to prepare for this important, exciting step in your career.

Benefits of Asking for a Raise versus Jumping Ship

One of the questions you must consider when thinking about your raise is whether you should ask for a raise or just look for a higher-paying job with another company entirely. While it may seem exciting to leave for another job that pays more, there are some good reasons to stay where you are, with a company where you have proved that you deserve to be paid more money.

If you are happy with your current job, it is usually in your best interest to stay where you are and lobby for more money. As you accrue more time at your current place of employment, you also accrue benefits. You may earn extra vacation days, opportunities for personal time off, and, possibly, the ability to apply for more lucrative positions within your company.

Leaving your company means you will have to start over with establishing your reputation and earning benefits, both of which come with company loyalty. Any accrued additional benefits at your current job will be lost when you move to another company. The relationships you have developed with your supervisors and coworkers will have to be re-formed with new people. You will have considerable work to do to re-assimilate yourself in a new corporate environment, and it is likely much of this work has already been done at your current job. Think carefully before giving up everything you have earned.

Additionally, you may not enjoy your new job as much as you enjoy your current job. Comfort and security at a job contribute considerably to satisfaction. You may end up trading one problem — such as wanting more money — for another problem, such as not enjoying your workplace.

Also remember that looking for work may take more time and effort than you expect. While you are devoting free time and energy looking for work, you may be losing money that you would have otherwise earned by asking for a raise at your current place of employment. Staying with your current job and securing a pay raise with your current employer will ultimately net you more money than stopping and starting again with a new company.

PART II
Getting Ready for Your Raise

Now that you understand the basics, it is time to start preparing to get your pay raise.

CHAPTER

4

Am I Where I Want to Be, and How Did I Get Here?

Before you know where you are going, you need to make sure you know where you currently are.

- Is this where you want to be in your career?
- How did you get to where you are?
- What are your future goals, and how will this job help you get there?

These are all questions that you need to have the answers to before you can move forward.

Regardless of where you are right now, picture your ideal job. The sky is the limit here. Ask yourself some questions:

- What does your office look like?

- What is your title?
- What are your daily responsibilities?
- How many people — if any — report to you?
- How many hours do you work?

These questions can be more difficult to answer than you may think. Maybe you are not sure of exactly what you want to do. Jobs are changing all the time, and this creates new opportunities for workers to express their professional goals. If you are having a hard time deciding what you want to do next, it will be helpful to look at where you have been.

The Past

The only way you can understand where you are currently is to recognize exactly where you have been. These questions will help you do just that — see where you have been and where you are now. Take some time to write out your answers. Writing your answers down will cause you to seriously consider them. To make the changes you are looking to make and earn your pay raise, you need to have solid answers ready.

What jobs have I had in the past?

List all the jobs you have held since you started working, regardless of whether you were 15 and working at an amusement park or fresh out of college. While you may be tempted to simply list your most recent jobs, it is important to go all the way back to the beginning.

If you have been working for a while, or have other obligations — like family — to deal with now, it is possible that you have made recent job choices based on perceived need rather than passion for the work. Describe each job you have had, why you took it, why you think you were hired, and how you felt about being there.

What did I like most about each of these jobs?

List everything you liked about each of these jobs individually, whether it was the co-workers, specific job duties, the location, the kind of chair you had, your office — everything. It is important to know exactly what you liked about these jobs so that you can truly understand what is most important to you. You may think that a certain salary or title is what counts, but your own patterns of work may suggest that a certain type of work environment and certain duties, regardless of title, are what are truly important to you. You can also begin to choose jobs that consist of the work that you like most.

What did I dislike about each of these jobs?

As with the previous question, list everything that turned you off about your past jobs, whether it was the types of clients that your company catered to, the hours you had to keep, or a set of tedious duties that you were expected to tend to. To successfully go after what you want, you will need to know what is in your best interest to avoid.

How well did I do at my jobs and why?

This is a moment to be absolutely honest with yourself. It will be important to know whether you did well or not. If you did well, then it may be safe to say that the work suited you. However, if you had any problems with a job, you will need to determine why you had those issues in the first place.

It could be that you were still developing your skills. Maybe you were uninterested in the work, and in turn, did not take the time to do the work well. Whatever the reason was, you need to be aware of it so you can apply this knowledge to work you will pursue in the future.

CASE STUDY: MIKE PRESLEY

Mike Presley
Store manager
Kingsport, Tennessee

Mike Presley, a store manager, says the most common mistake employees make when asking for a pay raise is not being prepared when asking for a raise if it is not time for the annual review.

He also says appearance is important when meeting to ask for a pay raise. Business casual is a minimum when meeting to request a raise, according to Presley.

A pay raise is warranted, Presley said, when an employee does the job asked of them and takes pride in doing it well. "They should be dependable and trustworthy. They should come to work on time and be flexible to meet company needs, within reason," said Presley.

Mistakes to avoid when asking for a raise include approaching the supervisor at a bad time or not being prepared for the meeting. Not scheduling an appointment and not being prepared results in a waste of time for both parties, he said.

Why did I leave these jobs?

People change jobs all the time. Employees move or need to change the number of hours they work.; they find other interests or receive better offers from other companies. Write down why you changed jobs:

- Did you have logistical concerns?
- Were you let go or laid off?
- Were you simply looking for something that better suited your interests?
- Were you scared to take the next step?
- Did a need of income push you toward taking something you did not want?
- Were you not skilled enough to take the job that you really desired?

The goal is not to judge your reasons for changing jobs, but rather, to identify what motivates you to make a change.

What did I do other than work?

Make a list of "extra-curricular" activities in which you have participated. These activities can include volunteer work, hobbies, or clubs in which you have held membership. Looking at how you spend your personal time can give you a better idea of what is most important to you and thus what will be most fitting to incorporate into your professional life.

Asking yourself about the past will aid you in seeing whether you are on a direct path toward your ideal job — or whether you will need to make some major adjustments toward the perfect career path.

The Present

Now that you have taken a trip down memory lane, it is time to look at where you are right now. This is the job that you are hoping to augment with a raise. Keep the journal out, and write down your thoughts on the following topics.

See whether you can create a linear path of jobs between your current job and where you want to go. If you have gotten off your ideal career path, reflect upon your past choices and analyze what actions caused you to veer. Whatever the reason is, do not beat yourself up about it; simply use what you have learned from your writing to determine what you need to do to get out of the rut and back on track toward your goals. Understanding what has held you back in the past will help you to avoid those same mistakes in the future. Once you know that you took a wrong turn, you can quickly get back on the road toward where you want to be in your career.

You may think that being on the wrong path means you need to abandon your job right now, or that asking for a raise will only trap you in a job that you are not interested in. If you are truly unhappy with your current position, then you certainly can consider leaving — but asking for a raise can be a strong method for righting your career.

With a raise comes added responsibility and additional attention from your employer. Because you will be discussing your career goals with your employer, you will have the chance to tell your boss where you want to go; then, the two of you can work toward that goal together.

Remember that regardless of where you are, you *can* get to where you want to be with the right amount of effort. Identify the strengths you possess in your current position that will help you in the next. Again, here are some questions to ask yourself:

What skills from your past jobs help you now?

Look at the jobs you have held previously. Regardless of whether they were in your current field, there are likely skills and experiences that can help you in your job today. Now is the time to list them. Having them in front of you will remind you that you harbor useful and relevant skills in your back pocket that can make your work better and stronger — and that will make you more likely to earn a raise.

Do you like the job you have?

Your attitude toward your current job may indicate how well you are doing it. If you are content with the job you have, you are more likely to be doing it well; if you do not, it is possible that you are letting your performance slip. You may not be doing this intentionally, but it can be a natural outcome of frustration with where you are in your career. What specific things do you like about your job?

- Do you like your boss and coworkers?
- Do you like the goals the company has for itself?
- What parts of your workday do you like best?

Knowing exactly what career aspects you like will help you identify your strengths, and pumping up these strengths will help you inch closer to getting your raise.

Because it is the present you are hoping to affect, it is the present you must understand. Take the time to answer the above questions. The more information you have about where you are, the better you will be able to navigate the path so you can reach your ideal destination.

The Future

Now that you have written about where you have been and where you presently are, it is time to look at where you want to move toward. It is not enough to say that you want "more money" or a "better job" one day. You need specific goals. The following questions will help you determine and definitively set your goals:

How do you see yourself in the company's future?

If you cannot see yourself as a part of the company's future, it is unlikely that your company sees you there, either. Regardless of what your position is now, to have professional success, you will need to be able to picture yourself climbing up your company's ladder.

What strengths would you like to use more often?

Determining which skills you enjoy using most will help you identify what kind of position will ultimately suit you best. If you enjoy using your creative skills more, then it will not be in your best interest to pursue a position that is strictly administrative, logistical, or number-crunching. Likewise, if you enjoy the technical aspects of your business, you should avoid taking a creative position simply because it may be available.

**What do you hope to achieve
in the next year or in the next five years?**

You may think these are trite, meaningless questions that employers ask during interviews to pass the time, but the answers to these questions are quite important. If you do not have goals to reach, you will have a hard time getting anywhere. Making decisions about what you would like to do will make it easier to advance.

To Review

It is crucial that you understand the basics of how businesses work before you begin to prepare to ask for your raise. Business is regulated in part by the government, in part by the demands of the company itself, and in part by what the company's employees stand for.

Setting compensation

As you look to change your compensation, you need to understand how your company arrived at your compensation rate in the first place. Companies consider the following criteria when setting salaries and wages.

- Supply and demand.

- How many people they need for a job, and how many people are available to do it.

- Job title, description, and overall duties.

- What exactly a job entails, from the specific work to the hours that the employee is expected to keep.

- What a job adds to a company. While every job brings something to a company, businesses are ultimately concerned with the bottom line — money. The more directly a position brings money into the company, the more that worker will likely be paid.

- The state of the economy. If the economy is doing well, businesses will feel more confident giving their employees more money. If the economy is slow, companies will be more likely to tighten their purse strings, and new hires may not have salaries as high as their predecessors.

- How the job has changed over time. With advances in technology, especially communication technology, jobs will become more sophisticated each year. The more sophisticated a job becomes, the higher the wages or salary for that particular job.

- The cost of living. Companies will set wages that are comparable to how much it costs to live where the company is located. Companies in expensive cities tend to pay their employees more to account for the expense of the city.

- What non-salary benefits come with the job. Companies may include non-pay benefits as part of an employee's compensation. There are many benefits companies could offer, and while these benefits do not result in direct pay to employees, they can pay in terms of savings or investments.

Moving forward

Despite all the rules and regulations involved in business, you should move forward with your plan to secure your raise. If you are doing good work, you deserve to be fairly compensated for it. Furthermore, setting and achieving goals, such as asking for and receiving a raise, will make you a stronger employee and a happier person.

You may be better served by asking for a raise than by looking for a new job. If you like the job you have and can visualize yourself climbing up its corporate ladder, asking for a raise is the stronger choice to make. Leaving your job may cause you to give up any benefits you have accrued over time, and there is no guarantee that you will make more than you are making now at a new company.

CHAPTER 5

Pay Raise Eligibility

J ust because you want a raise does not mean that you are ready for it — or that you deserve it. This next section will help you determine whether you are genuinely ready to request one. You certainly do not want to ask before you are sincerely ready. If you ask prematurely, you will not only lose out on your raise, but you will also have a difficult time shaking the impression that you have created for yourself. Now that you know what your company is looking for, use the following section to see whether you meet standard eligibility requirements.

Gauging Your Eligibility

Before you begin preparing yourself to request a raise, you must know whether you are in a position that would make you eligible for a raise. When companies consider rewarding someone with an increase in pay, they look at several key questions:

How many people can do this employee's job?

If many people can do the job, the employee will not be a strong candidate for a raise. If a job is highly specialized, it will be more likely that the company will consider this employee someone whom it is willing to reward with a raise.

What is the average rate for this job across the market?

If an employee is already making what other similar employees at other companies are making, that employee will be less likely to easily convince the powers that be that he or she deserves more money. But if an employee's salary does not match up with industry standards, a company may feel more apt to give that employee a raise.

How much does the company value this employee?

There are certain criteria that will make an employee more valuable as an individual. These attributes may include:

- Professional awards or recognition
- Membership in prestigious organizations
- Personal relationships with higher-ranking employees
- Strong professional connections
- High status at a previous place of employment

If an employee does not meet the above criteria, that does not mean he or she is out of the running for a raise, but it would be in an employee's best interest to add some cachet to his or her résumé.

Are other companies interested in this employee?

The business world is competitive, and if other offices are looking to hire an employee from a company, the company will perhaps start to realize that this employee is indeed a valuable worker.

Has this employee made the company money?

The bottom line is that businesses are about making money, and before a company is willing to give more money to an employee, it will need to feel confident that the employee will make them more money in the future. If the employee has made the company money before, the company can feel confident that the employee can do it again.

Ask yourself these questions

The following questions will help you determine where you are in relation to your raise. Nothing about these questions was written to discourage you from pursuing your pay goals. The questions and their explanations are simply meant to give you a clear, honest idea of how your employer sees you. Immediately following the questions are ways to increase your eligibility and put yourself on the path toward your raise:

Am I unique?

Companies value having employees with unique skill sets; therefore, if you are one of several employees who are essentially doing the same job, it is less likely that an employer will look favorably upon you as someone who commands a raise. Conversely, if you are the only person in your position, or only a few employees have your full list of responsibilities, you will be more likely to easily petition for a raise.

To most accurately answer the question "Am I unique?" you need to take stock of where you fit into the company's profile. Find out how many people do your job. You can ask your supervisor, go to the human resources department, or take a best-guess head count as you walk through your office. You do not need to know an exact number, but you do need to have a good idea of how many people share your title.

Can I manage others?

It is likely that your raise will come with increased responsibility and higher expectations from your employer. If a company gives an employee a raise, they are also committing to keep that employee at the company longer. If your company sees you as someone who can rise up the ranks and take the next step to being a manager or having some sort of supervisory position, it is more likely that the company will invest in you by giving you a raise.

If you have managed a staff of any size before, you should look at what your record was like when you did. Did your team help increase revenue? Were your staff members happy with your performance as their supervisor? Were you able to court a high-level employee for your team?

If you have not managed others before, you and your employer will both have to evaluate your potential to manage others. Some traits that signify a good manager in the making are:

- Excellent written and verbal communication skills
- Time management ability
- The ability to be an active, effective listener
- The ability to delegate efficiently

- Complete understanding of the job
- Insight into the workings of the business

Have my duties changed since I was hired?

Employers like to see employees who are doing things that other employees are not. The more new duties you take on as your time at your job continues, the more unique you will appear in your employer's eye — and thus, the more likely you will be to get your raise.

When you started your job, you were likely given a list of job duties that you were expected to perform. If you were not given a physical list, you should be able to procure your official job description from your supervisor or your human resources department. This list will let you know whether your job duties have changed.

It is not enough to know that your duties have changed. Your duties will need to have increased in responsibility or difficultly. If any changes to your workload have been lateral in nature, rather than vertical, the answer to the question, "Have my duties changed since I was hired?" is essentially "No." To put yourself in the best position to earn a raise, you should be doing more work on top of the work you were hired to do, or more difficult work than was agreed upon when you were hired.

Will another company pay me more?

This question affects your petition for a raise from two angles. First, if the going rate for your job is higher than what you are currently receiving for it from your employer, then your company likely owes you a raise. Second, if another company simply values you more than your company does, this information will likely cause your company to re-evaluate how they have been previously critiquing you, and possibly give you a raise when they do.

To address the first angle of this question, look into what the going rate for your job is at other companies. You can find this information from a variety of resources:

- Union and trade publications. Unions conduct regular surveys to stay on top of what their members are earning at work.

- Various compensation-related Web sites, including:
  - **www.Jobstar.org**
  - **www.Salary.com**
  - **www.Payscale.com**

- The Occupational Outlook Handbook, published every two years by the U.S. Department of Labor. You can find it in book form in most libraries or bookstores, or you can use it online for free at **www.bls.gov/oco**.

Addressing the second angle of this question may require some more clandestine work. If you have been courted for an interview, you will be able to get this information first hand and can use it — not maliciously, of course — when you go to your boss to ask for your raise. If you currently are not looking to change jobs, you may want to schedule some informational interviews to get an idea of what you might make working for another company.

An informational interview is an interview between a worker and a business where there is no expectation of hiring. It is a chance for employees to find out about the working environment, workload, and pay for a job they may have an interest in some time in the future. It is also a chance for a company to show off their best assets and court potential talent without having to worry about bringing someone onboard.

Whether you find out what another company may pay you for your job from independent sources or directly from another employer, it is important to know whether they will pay you more. If they will, this may cause your perceived value to rise in your employer's eyes — and thus, this can become valuable information to bring to your employer when asking for your raise.

Can I show them the money?

When it comes to money, you will need to show your employer that a) you have helped the company make more money, and that b) giving you a raise will help the company make even more money.

There are some jobs in which it is fairly easy to determine whether you have contributed to the company's bottom line. If you are in sales, marketing, or advertising, it will be an easy task to track how your work has added to company revenue. Likewise, if you are an executive, it will be simple to track your client's work to see how it has added to the company. On the other hand, if you do a job that is clerical or administrative in nature, or if you work in retail — where your work is not measured in terms of a commission — it may be more difficult to determine what you have done that has increased the company's coffers.

If your job is not one that directly causes revenue to increase, then you need to find other, creative ways of showing that your work has added to the bottom line. The following are some common types of jobs and how you can help show whether work done in that position actually helped increase company profits:

- **Assistant.** Keeping a higher-ranking employee(s) organized allows them to do their job more efficiently, and, in turn, adds to company revenue.

- **Receptionist.** Maintaining a professional, friendly presence for clients makes those clients feel more comfortable with the business. The more comfortable they are from the moment they enter the business, the more comfortable they will be spending their money there.

- **Retail sales associate.** Attending to customers in a professional, helpful manner will make those customers more likely to spend their money.

- **Customer service representative.** The more an employee can help a customer feel comfortable with where they are purchasing and the items they are purchasing, the more likely those customers will be to buy from that business — and to return to it. Even when dealing with initially negative conversations, like a complaint or a return, a skilled customer service representative will handle the situation in such a way that both customer and company win.

Do I know the company policy for requesting a raise?

This is a simple question that many raise-seekers overlook, but one that is necessary to answer. Review your company's policy handbook, speak with the human resources department, or chat with your supervisor to find out what the company policy is for requesting changes in your job status. You may find that your company will only hear a case for a raise after a certain period of employment, or that the person you were planning on going to is not the person who handles these decisions. You may learn that you need to submit your request to a number of people. Whatever the policy is, ensure you are familiar with it so you do not waste your time and lose your chance for a raise based on a minor technicality.

Find out the specifics of what you have to do to earn a raise. While the steps in this book will help you stand out as an employee and put you in a stronger position for your raise, there may be criteria that are company-specific. You will need to be aware of them so you do not leave out a crucial step in your quest for a raise. Speak with your supervisor or human resources department to learn the exact criteria.

Does my company know where I am going?
Will a raise help me get there?

For the most part, companies want their employees to be around for a while. High turnover rates are not good for business because it reflects upon them negatively and wastes their time and resources. When a company invests money in an employee through their initial hire rate, benefits, and raises, the company will want to be sure it is making an investment in a sure thing. If your professional goals are in-line with the company's ideas for you, you will be more likely to be at the company longer. This will please your company and make you more likely to procure a raise. Of course, the only way for your employer to know where you want to go is if they hear it from you.

Taking inventory of your professional goals is important to do on a regular basis. That way, you can easily find out whether you are wasting your company's or your own time and money. If you cannot get to where you want to go through your current position, it may be time to look for a new position, rather than making yourself more indebted to your current company. Figuring out where you want to go and whether your current employer can get you there is not selfish; it is simply good business sense, which you and your employer will appreciate in the long run.

Receiving a raise means that a company wants to have you around longer. You will likely receive more responsibilities and become a higher-profile employee. More than one person will almost certainly have to sign off on your raise, and all those involved will want to take a good look at you.

You should be aware that jumping ship shortly after you are rewarded with more money will make it difficult for you to get a good recommendation to take with you to a new job. A raise may also come with a change in your contract, making it more difficult for you to leave your current employer quickly or without penalty.

A raise may not be what you actually deserve right now. Take some time to review your professional goals. If a raise is what will help get you to the next level in your career, then read on and collect the money you honestly feel you deserve.

Review your answers to these questions:

- Am I unique?
- Can I manage others?
- Have my duties changed since I was hired?
- Can I show how I have helped the company make money?
- Will another company pay me more?
- Do I know the company policy for requesting a raise?
- Do I know where I am going? Will a raise get me there?

Chances are, you have more than one "No" on this list, and if you are just beginning your quest for a raise, you may have several. But read on to find out how to turn "No" into "Yes" and put yourself on the path to successfully earning your raise.

After you understand what companies consider when looking to give an employee a raise, you need to ask yourself the same questions to evaluate your own eligibility. Because a raise may come with increased responsibility, you will need to know whether you can handle it. Being able to manager other employees will put you in a strong position to earn a raise. If you have not managed others before, the following are skills that you should exhibit:

- Strong written and verbal communication skills
- Time management
- Effective listening
- The ability to delegate
- Comprehensive understanding of your job and field
- Insight into the business

Have my duties changed since I was hired?

If you are doing exactly what you were doing when you were hired, you will have a more difficult time explaining why you should receive more money. If you have steadily taken on more responsibility and shown that you can rise to the occasion, you will have an easier time showing evidence of why you deserve a raise.

Will another company pay me more?

Your salary should be comparable to what others in your position are making at other companies. If you find that another company will pay you more to do what you do for your own employer, your employer may be convinced to look favorably upon your raise request.

Can I show them the money?

If you can easily show how your doing your job has helped your company make money, you will be in a strong position to negotiate a raise. If you are not sure how your job has helped the company earn money, you need to take some time to figure that out. Even if you are not directly responsible for sales or customer service, you can probably find a concrete way that doing your job well contributes to the company's bottom line.

Do I know the company policy for requesting a raise?

Avoid working against yourself by doing things against protocol. Check with your company's human resources department to make sure you go about requesting your raise the way your company prefers.

**Does my company know where I am going,
and will a raise get me there?**

If your employer does not think that you have a vested interest in remaining loyal to and growing with your company, you may have a difficult time convincing him or her that you deserve a raise.

Spend some time evaluating your own career goals.

- **The past:** Where you have been will explain the reasons why you are where you currently are.

- **The present:** Make sure you are using your skills and experience as efficiently as you can. Maybe you have gotten off track, or maybe you are right where you want to be. Either way, understanding the present will help you take the next step.

- **The future:** Determine where you want to be, what skills you want to use, and how you see yourself in your company's future. Have a conversation with your boss to discuss your goals so both of you will be on the same page.

CHAPTER 6

Mastering the Basics

To master the basics of your career, you must work effectively and efficiently. To do this, you must have your workspace well-organized, and you must have the ability prioritize work, manage distractions, and master the basics of being professional. Appropriate dress and looking the part of an executive climbing the ladder is also important in your success.

Workspace Organization

The first step toward doing your work well is being organized. Keeping your workspace neat and your work in order makes any job easier. With proper organization skills, you will make fewer mistakes and be in a better position to correct mistakes that are almost inevitably going to be occasionally made. Your increased efficiency will make you stand out and put you one step closer to your raise.

Organizing your desk or workspace

Whether you clock in hours in your own office, a cubicle, an open-area desk, or a universal work area, keeping your workspace tidy and organized is the first step toward organizing all your work. This is where you will spend most of your time, so it has the potential for becoming cluttered. A clean, organized desk will not only make you look better; it will also make you work better and perform more efficiently. Keep it tidy with the following steps:

Clean off before you clean out. Remove everything from the top of your workspace and clean off the surface of your desk. Dust and clean the surface with a cleaner. When your physical desk looks clean, it will only enhance the organization you do on top of it.

Give loose personal items — such as your cell phone, keys, and wallet — a dedicated area on your desk, in a drawer, or in a locker. Do not leave these items strewn about your desktop. It is possible that leaving them out will attract office thieves, and they will also potentially become mixed in with your papers, pens, and work documents.

Find a hidden area where you can keep these items all day without having to move them. This area should be away from your main work area; this way, you will always know where to find them if you need them. These items will also be safe from nosy eyes and wandering hands. If you do not have a drawer or other hidden storage place, consider purchasing a small storage box for these items. You can leave the box on your desk, and your items will be safer than they would be if they were loosely left on your desk.

Limit the number of pens, pencils, highlighters, and other writing instruments you keep at your work area. If you have any pens or highlighters that are out of ink, throw them away. If you have mechanical pencils for which you do not have refills, or standard pencils that are worn down to their nubs, throw them away as well.

Likewise, if you have more than a few pens and pencils, return them to a central office supply location. You can only use one writing instrument at a time, and there is no reason to have dozens of extras at your immediate disposal. They take up space and contribute to clutter.

Hide wires. Any cord that connects any electronic device — your computer, phone charger, and others — to its power source should be routed so it does not travel across your workspace. Many desks come with small holes in the back through which to thread these wires. If your desk or workspace does not have such an opening, use small pieces of electrical tape to secure the wires to the back edge of your desk. This will keep your wires from getting crossed and becoming a confusing bundle of cords. It will also keep these stray items out of your way.

Keep what you use closest to you. If you regularly take notes at meetings and need notepads, then your notepads should be kept close to you at your workspace so you can grab them quickly. If you regularly need certain reference books, keep those close as well. In other words, whatever items you need most often should be within arm's reach. Move items that you do not need often to lower drawers or the farthest edges of your desk. This will prevent you from having to sort through extraneous material to get to what you need.

Organizing paperwork

Paperwork is the No. 1 cause of clutter. Much of what goes on in a business is printed on paper, then distributed company-wide. The notes, letters, and memos end up in huge piles on desks. You should take care to keep this paper pile at a minimum. Not only will it help prevent a fire hazard, but it will also allow you to efficiently tackle the jobs that need to be done and avoid wasting your time on paper that belongs in the recycling bin.

Create a filing system. Filing cabinets or drawers with hanging files are an indispensable resource. They are simple to use, and provide quick access to your paperwork. They can be easily rearranged, and if someone else needs to get something from your desk, it will be much easier for them to find that item in a file folder system than if they have to root through undifferentiated papers on your desk.

To create your file system, use hanging folders with tabs as your first level of organization, and then file folders with tabs as the next level of organization. Make sure to label your tabs clearly so you can easily find what you need. Do not over-fill the file folders, as that only makes it more difficult to flip through the pages and find what you need.

Here are some sample sections you can create in your filing system:

- To Do Today
- Contacts
- Special Projects
- Invoices and Receipts
- Letterheads and Forms
- Returned Correspondence

Your "To Do Today" file should be kept on your desk where it can be clearly seen and referenced.

Take the time to decide whether to keep an item. Every time you are presented with a new piece of paper — an office memo, a letter, or whatever it may be — read it immediately. If it is something that does not pertain to you, throw it away right then, or recycle it. If there is simple information in the document — like a phone number, e-mail address, or date for an event — transfer this information to your address book or calendar immediately, then throw away the paper or recycle it. The point of this is to immediately get rid of paper that you do not need. If the paper is something that needs to be kept for reference, such as a company phone list or a returned piece of correspondence, it should be immediately filed away accordingly.

If the paper contains questions you need to answer or issues you need to address, read through it again, this time with a highlighter. Highlight the parts of the document that require your attention. On the top of the page, write the date and time by which these concerns must be addressed; this will help you prioritize your work. You should also record in your calendar or day planner the same information about your deadline. If you are unable to immediately attend to the matter, file the paper where it will be easily accessible and where you will not forget to handle it.

At the end of the day, review any stray papers you may have on your desk. Before you go home, you should make sure to throw away or recycle any papers you do not need anymore. Leaving your desk clutter-free will put you in a better position to start your day off strong the next morning.

Scan documents and store them as digital files. Small pieces of paperwork, like receipts, can be hard to keep up with — even in a filing system. Their small size makes them easy to misplace, or they may get caught up in the folds, creases, staples, and bindings of larger documents. One way to alleviate this problem is to use a document scanner to create a digital file of your receipt. Once a document is scanned, you can burn the information onto a CD or other storage device, or directly store it on your hard drive. Before tossing a receipt, though, double-check to make sure you will not need the original.

Scanning documents is also a convenient way to store paperwork that you do not think you will need in the future, but do not want to lose completely. Computers come with a variety of storage options. You can store your information directly onto the computer's drive, onto a CD or other media, or onto an external drive. Your company may even have drives set aside especially for document storage. Check with your IT department to find out what your digital storage options are.

At the end of every week, go through your files. Review what paperwork is still in them and whether they are still relevant. Throw away or recycle anything that no longer needs your attention, or papers that have old or expired information, such as old contact lists. Make sure any receipts are turned over to the appropriate department for safekeeping.

Francine Russell, a personal assistant, offers her advice for staying organized at work. "Clutter occurs because things don't have a designated place," she said. "When you don't know where to put something, you tend to just leave it lying around."

For example, what likely happens when you pick up a piece of paper from your mailbox? You do not have a good place to file it, but it is important and you do not want to lose it, so you put it back in the mailbox because at least then you will know where to find it again.

The obvious problem, Russell said, is that the mailbox is soon overflowing, and is no longer current with new items coming in to your workspace. When you do need that important piece of paper again, you have now got a huge stack of "important" papers to dig through to find it.

As the papers multiply, the idea of organizing them becomes overwhelming, she said. At some point, you have to just set aside a day or two to clear your desk and put everything away. It is exhausting, but afterward, you feel good — until that mailbox starts growing again.

You need a system for dealing with the paper, and you need to work that system every day; that is key. There is no other answer to the clutter problem. People hoard unneeded material because they are afraid that someday, they are going to need it — or they do not trust their ability to sort the important from the trivial.

Overall, people tend to have way too much stuff. So much, in fact, that it has led to the creation of a whole new job market: the professional organizer. Most organizers will tell you that much of their job involves telling clients, "Throw it away."

Start small. When the mail comes, immediately toss all the junk fliers. Then open the bills, tossing the envelopes and all those extra inserts, and even the return envelope, if you know you will be paying electronically. Then do the same with the rest of the mail, so that all you are left with are the important documents that require action. You will likely find it is a small pile, and that almost two-thirds of what came in the mail is garbage.

As you get better with handling the mail, you can start applying this technique to your files and that mess on your desk. Go through your drawers and only keep a reasonable amount of office supplies; give away the surplus.

The more you throw away, the more comfortable you become with letting go of things — and the better you get at making the decision about what to keep and what to toss. Most people find this quite liberating.

Filing paperwork

There are two good criteria: File papers so you can find them when needed, and file papers so that someone else — like your boss — can also find what is needed without too much trouble.

Items that are related should be filed together in the same place. Filing everything alphabetically rarely works well; better to file them by project or client.

Hanging file folders keep files together and keep them from sliding around in a drawer. A printed label — never hand-written — on the hanging file folder announces the project or client. Purchase the 3.5-inch tabs instead of using the short ones that come with the hanging folders.

Inside the hanging folder, place the files that go with that project. Use two lines when labeling files: the first line, in small type, should include the name of the project or client, while the second line, in larger type, should announce the contents of the file — for example, "Purchase Orders," "Correspondence," or "Deal Memos."

This way, if the file gets left out somewhere, it is easy to tell just by looking at the label which project/client it goes with and what is inside the file. You can also have a "pending" section — a place to keep things that you are working on right now.

And think ahead; if you needed to find this file or piece of paper in the future, the first place you would look for it is where you file it. A trait of a good organizational system is that you can put your hands on what you need immediately.

If you do look for something and it is in the second or third place you look, consider re-filing it in the first location. Feel free to modify your system as you go along. Experience will teach you what is working and what is not.

Color-coding can also be useful. For example, use green files for bills and receipts, yellow files for correspondence, and red files for legal documents. Then, when you open your file drawer and go to the section for a particular client or project, it is easy to pull the "Billing" (green) or the "Legal" (red) file.

Keep a piece of paperwork if it provides backup for some business expense that your company writes off on its taxes, or if it is a receipt for a business purchase, lunch, or event. The main reason we save much of what we do is to prove our case to the IRS if we are audited. Learn what you need to keep for this type of backup, and file it away by year.

If a piece of paper provides legal proof of something — such as the date that a request was made, or the fact that a person agreed to something — then keep it. If the proof you want to save is contained in an e-mail, print the e-mail. Do not trust that you will be able to retrieve an electronic communication three or four years down the road.

Contact information — such as names, addresses, companies, and titles — should be transferred to your database, and then toss the paper, letter, or business card.

To help them get organized, some people like files, some like binders, and some like baskets. Anything works, as long as you can easily put your hands on any piece of information you need quickly.

Labels are valuable. They allow you to determine what is in a file, binder, or basket without riffling through every piece of paper. Color can also be useful in separating out files or projects, or highlighting different jobs on a calendar.

An up-to-date database helps you manage contacts. The good thing about most computer databases is that they allow you to search by name, company, or category — this is much more efficient than flipping through a stack of business cards.

Everyone needs a "To Do" list — some method for writing down things that need to be done, and then checking them off. The goal with a "To Do" list is that nothing falls through the cracks.

Do not trust your memory; write everything down. Please remember that sticky notes stuck on every available surface, or scraps of paper with cryptic scribbles in your wallet, do not count. Write all your "to dos" in one central, safe place. Calendaring systems tend to be best. Microsoft's Outlook program or a paper appointment book will allow you to write "to dos" on the actual date that they need to be done, even if it is two months down the road.

But remember that you need to reference that list every day. Writing it all down somewhere and then never looking at it again does not work.

Phone and E-mail Message Organization

Phone calls and e-mails can easily get lost in the shuffle of the day, so you will need to have a plan for tracking these forms of communication. Doing so will keep you on top of your work — and at the top of the list for a raise.

Phone messages

Dedicate one notepad to your phone messages. This will prevent your messages from getting confused with other information you write down. You can use a standard notepad or purchase a notepad that has pre-printed sections for the various parts of a phone message.

When taking a message, be sure to get several pieces of information, including the return phone number, the full message, and the date and time by which the call needs to be returned or the matter needs to be resolved. Always gather all this information, even if you know the contact well. Getting all the necessary details as soon as you can prevents you from having to make additional follow-up calls before completing the work.

If you did not take the message, but are getting the information off of your voicemail, record all of the aforementioned information. If a piece of the information is missing, immediately call your contact back and ask for what is missing. Calling immediately will prevent you from forgetting any part of the message or assignment.

Track your messages on your dedicated notepad. As you get more information about the assignment or issue, record it on the notepad; that way, you will have all information easily accessible when you return the call.

E-mail

You should treat e-mail in a similar way to your piles of paperwork. When you get a new e-mail message, you should read it to see whether it contains information that you need to tend to immediately, or whether you can simply transfer some information quickly before deleting the e-mail. Just like you keep your desktop clear of extraneous paper, you will also want to keep your e-mail inbox clear of unnecessary e-mail.

If an e-mail requires attention, print it out or use your e-mail system to highlight the e-mail. Record the date and time by which the e-mail needs a response, and plan accordingly. It may be helpful to print your e-mail and record information on the paper like you would in your phone message notebook. Properly file this paper, as you do not want it to create extra clutter.

Whether it is a company-distributed letter, a phone message, or an e-mail, you will want to avoid hanging on to these documents longer than necessary. There is an acronym in business called OHIO: Only Handle It Once. This means you should immediately decide what to do with a piece of paper and do it, instead of holding on to the paper and regularly saying that you will get around to it. Using the OHIO method will keep your desk clutter-free and your work in better condition, which increases your chances of getting a pay raise.

Work Prioritization

Regardless of your position or title, prioritizing your work is crucial to being an effective employee. If you do work quickly, but take too long to get to the most important tasks, your energy expenditure will be woefully inefficient. If you take care of the important tasks, but do not have any energy leftover for the less exciting — but still important — tasks, the glory you get from the big project will be short-lived. Therefore, it is necessary to understand how to prioritize the work that needs to be done to make sure you get to all of it and complete it to the best of your ability.

Make a list, check it twice

Write down a list of tasks you need to complete with the date and time by which they need to be completed. Make this list as comprehensive as possible. Include what you need to get done that day, that week, and that month. You need to have a clear idea of what the total list is so you can attend to it all.

Break tasks into steps. It is not enough to say, "Finish Thompson report." You will need to include the steps necessary to finish the Thompson report. This may involve interviewing a client, researching a project, or doing some data entry. Writing down all these steps will give you a clearer picture of what you need to do. A portion of your task list should look something like this:

Finish Thompson Report – Friday, 4/18/00, 3 p.m.

- Check invoices against receipts
- Budget final step of project
- Call John Thompson for approval of budget

Update team contact list – Tuesday (tomorrow) 4/15/09, 11 a.m.

- Collect contact info via e-mail

Schedule lunch with Susan Chavez – Monday, 4/21/09, noon

Return phone call from Margaret Lucas – Today – 5 p.m.

Attend April birthday breakfast – Wednesday, 4/23/09 – 10 a.m.

After you have your list, you will be able to immediately prioritize by date and time, but there are still other factors to take into consideration. You will need to determine how much time each step toward your task will take. If the individual steps are time-consuming, then you will need to raise their priority so you have time to complete them. You will also need to consider whether you need to rely on others to help you complete these tasks. If so, you will need to raise the priority so you can take into account waiting on someone else's schedule in addition to your own.

Re-prioritize as necessary. As plans change and tasks come and go, you will need to re-evaluate your priority list. An emergency item may come up, and you should attend to what becomes most urgent. Later, we will discuss how to address changes in your priorities list with your supervisor. Change is necessary, and priorities will change. Nevertheless, if you keep your priority list up-to-date, you will always be ready to handle change.

Working Efficiently

Once you have your work area organized and your task list prioritized, you can move on to finding ways to get your work done efficiently. All the organization in the world will not help you if you get held up by actually getting the work done. Next, we will discuss ways to work more efficiently and speed up your raise.

Stress is not always bad

Each day you are at work, you have designated tasks to accomplish. You have important duties that need to be completed, and people who are counting on your work. If you begin to think that the work you are doing is not important, or that the tasks that need to be completed are not urgent, you will be doing your work and yourself a disservice. Though you do not want to over-stress yourself, use these daily stressors to your advantage. Use them to keep your guard up and your sense of urgency intact.

Learning to make stress actually work for you will not only help you get your work done, but it will make you look good. When your employers and supervisors see that you are taking the work they give you seriously, they will appreciate your attitude. They will think more highly of you than the employee who casually moves through his or her tasks.

There are some ways to make sure you remember that all the work you are doing is important:

- **Keep your task list where you can clearly see it.** This will remind you of the work that needs to be done. As you check items off your list, you will feel encouraged to keep going.

- **Allow co-workers to follow up with you.** When you know you will receive a phone call or e-mail asking about what you are working on, you will be motivated to move through the work quickly so you will be able to give them a good report.

- **Keep your personal goals high.** As you make your task list, do not just record the bare minimum. Give yourself plenty to do in a day. The more you achieve, the better you will feel about yourself, and the more you will be inspired to do.

Of course, you do not want to sacrifice quality as you move quickly through your tasks. Take time to review your work before submitting it, or put it aside and then move to another task. When you have completed the second task, go back to the previous one and review it for mistakes or items you may have forgotten. The break will let you clear your head to see the previous items more clearly. Reviewing your material will allow you to be sure you are presenting the best work you can. When your work is the best it can be, and you have worked toward completing it with urgency, your employers will notice your efforts and be more likely to grant you your well-deserved raise.

Save and back up your material

Avoid that horrible feeling in the pit of your stomach when your computer crashes and the last few hours of your work disappear into the digital ether. Often, this material can be recovered with a certain amount of work and time, but it is much better to not have to worry about any potential loss. To make sure your work does not get lost, you should get into the habit of saving your work regularly.

Many computer programs come with an auto-save function. Consult the help section of your various programs or your company's IT department to find out how to use the auto-save functions to your advantage. These programs will regularly copy active files that you are working on and save them to a predetermined space on your computer's hard drive, providing a safety net in case of a computer crash.

A computer is just a machine, however, and just as you cannot rely solely on the spell-check programs to catch all your mistakes, you cannot count on an auto-save program to do all your back-up work. You can use two keystrokes to save your work every few seconds: Ctrl + S (or Command + S on Apple computers).

Saving your work every paragraph or every few minutes may seem like overkill, but your computer simply overwrites the previous file, so it does not take up any extra space in the memory. And a keystroke only takes a second to use, so it does not take up any extra time in your workday. A lost file, however, will take considerable time and effort to replace. Get into the habit of backing up your work, and you will not have to worry about losing time or effort. Your boss and clients will appreciate the fact that the work you do for them is safe from computer malfunction.

In addition to saving your work on the computer that you do your work on, you should also back up your material to an external device that is separate from your computer. You can save your work to a CD or an external hard drive. Speak to your company about providing these things for you. It is possible that your IT department has external drives available for you to store your work on, or you may be able to use your company's internal intranet system to send your work to an additional location. With this kind of protection, you can work comfortably, knowing that you will always be able to get to your work when you need to.

Be ready for inspiration

You never know when you might conjure up an idea for work. Solutions to complex problems often come to us when our minds are busy doing something else entirely. You may be at home having dinner, in the shower, watching television, or dreaming. Get into the habit of carrying a small notebook and pens with you so that you can record ideas as they come.

Writing down your ideas and thoughts about your work also gives you the chance to work through items more completely. Psychologists have suggested that journaling can help people work out problems. Writing uses a different part of the brain than thinking alone and can inspire thinking differently about a problem. If you carry writing tools with you at all times, you will be ready when inspiration strikes, and you will give yourself another means through which to work out problems.

Manage distractions

Your workday will be filled with all kinds of distractions, many of which you cannot control, such as an unexpected fire drill in the office, a last-minute meeting, or a call from an angry client. These distractions may take you away from your work and cause you to work less efficiently. Because there are plenty of circumstances you cannot control, make sure to control the ones you can. This will help you get your work done faster and better — and will impress those in charge of granting you your raise.

Turn off e-mail alerts

Many e-mail providers also provide a series of chimes and chirps to let you know that you have a new e-mail in your inbox. This is typically helpful, unless you are trying to get other work done. The constant aural reminder that you have new e-mail can be more distracting than helpful, especially if your e-mail is suspect to SPAM of any kind. You should turn off the reminder sound, unless you are expecting something urgent.

Instead of relying on the sound, designate a regular time when you will check your e-mail. You can decide to do this once an hour, or maybe two or three times a day, if your e-mail is not urgent. Letting messages collect in your inbox instead of reading each one as it comes in will allow you to better concentrate on the tasks you are doing. Checking your e-mail in batches will also allow you to handle several e-mails at once, which is more efficient than shifting focus every few minutes to answer the latest online missive.

Additionally, answering batches of e-mails will allow you to better focus on the e-mails when you do answer. Because your focus is not being split between the task on your desk and the e-mail, you will be able to devote all your attention to the e-mail. You will also not have to shuffle through extraneous papers or files to find what you need to answer the e-mail.

Turn off personal cell phone

Your personal cell phone can be a significant distraction during the workday. Turning it off will limit its pull on you. Family members and friends can wait until your lunch break or the end of the workday to talk to you. If there is a true emergency, they can always call your office phone.

Keeping your phone off will also prevent you from finding other ways to distract yourself with it. You will not be tempted to look at those cute pictures you just took of your dog that morning, or to quickly text your friend about dinner Friday night. And the more focused you are on your work, the better your work will be.

Limit personal calls

Though you definitely have the power to prevent yourself from making personal phone calls during the day, you do not have the same power to prevent people from calling you on your work phone to discuss non-work matters. If this happens, you should end the call as quickly as possible. Your friends will understand that you are busy at work, and your employer will appreciate that you respect their time enough to stick to business matters when you are in their office.

If a work call turns into a personal chat, you will need to end that call quickly as well. Aside from the fact that having a leisurely conversation about something other than the task at hand takes up valuable time, it also distracts from your work. When you end the personal call, it may take you many minutes to refocus your efforts back on your work. If you take personal calls too often, those minutes will turn into considerable time wasted on the job.

Arrive early or stay late

It is often easiest to get work done when no one else is around. When the office is quiet, you can be free from all distractions. The best way to find this time is to arrive shortly before the bulk of the staff or stay a little longer, after they are gone. You may only need an hour or half an hour of alone time to significantly increase your production. Then, you will be freer during the rest of the day to attend to the rest of the things on your to-do list.

Your employer will likely appreciate the extra time. Bosses like to see a hard worker, and one of the easiest ways to show that you are dedicated to the job is to be there when no one else is. This does not mean that you should overwork yourself and sacrifice all free time, but 30 extra minutes or so at the beginning or end of the day can make a large difference in how you are perceived and put you on the path to earning your raise.

Make friends later

Just as you need to limit personal phone calls, you will also need to limit personal conversations at the office. If a co-worker comes by and wants to discuss something other than work, you will need to end that conversation as quickly as possible. Politely tell them that you have work to do and will need to get back to it quickly. Your co-worker should understand that work duties need to be attended to at work. You will have plenty of time to connect during lunch or over drinks after work. If your co-worker pushes the issue of talking, suggest an after-hours meal or other get-together to connect.

Preventing idle talk at work helps you in a few ways: It allows you to focus more completely on the work that needs attention in order to be finished; it shows your boss that you have appropriate work boundaries; and it helps prevent you from getting caught up in office gossip.

Limit breaks

Most unions tell their signatory agencies that their members are entitled to a certain number of breaks each day. Breaks are important. They allow you to momentarily clear your head before diving back into difficult assignments; give you a chance to handle personal matters, such as a quick phone call or e-mail; give you a chance to get a snack or drink to revive you; and give you a few minutes to catch up with co-workers.

However, breaks should be taken judiciously. Watch how long you are spending on your breaks. If you take more than 15 minutes, you are taking advantage of the time. Consider your break a time to get refreshed and ready to continue tackling the business of the day, and not an hour to do whatever you want while your work waits for you on your desk.

Keep a Positive Attitude

We have discussed that your work should be done well — that it should be error-free, delivered on time, and to the proper specifications. However, if you are turning in good work with a negative, belligerent, or elitist attitude, your hard work may be overlooked because of your personal presentation. Your attitude and the demeanor with which you approach your work are just as important as the work itself.

A positive attitude does not mean keeping a fake smile plastered to your face — although a sincere smile certainly does not hurt in most situations. A positive attitude is simply that — looking at situations from a positive point of view.

Maybe your boss just assigned you a boring or mundane task to do. Maybe you have just been asked to work late or to come in early to finish a special project. Maybe someone else slacked off on his or her work, and now the overflow has fallen to your desk. Maybe a project is taking longer than you had planned or hoped for it to take, and it is eating into your own free time. It would be easy to look at each of these situations with a negative attitude; it would be simple, expected, and — in many cases — understandable to complain about these situations or to try to get out of dealing with them. But when working your way up the corporate ladder, you do not want to do what is expected. You want to rise above and take action that is proactive, positive, and that moves situations toward solutions.

It is true that attitude can be evaluated subjectively. There will be some people who may just not warm to you for reasons you may not understand and cannot control. Even so, you should take care to employ behaviors that can be defined as pleasant and positive. Although you cannot please everyone, you can take proactive steps to make sure most people see that your attitude is an optimistic one.

Challenges are just opportunities in disguise

In your average day at an average office, any number of things may go wrong — everything from a copy jam to an employee walking out on a project. Anything could happen, and with the right attitude, you will be ready for anything. If you look at problems from this point of view, you will see that problems and challenges are actually opportunities for you to prove your business acumen. Solutions you come up with to see any problems or issues can be used to show off your strengths and talents. However, you can only show off these characteristics if you keep the right attitude.

Let us look at the problems mentioned a few paragraphs ago. Any of those issues may come up during an average day at the office. At first blush, they may seem like annoying problems, but — with some creative thinking — you can turn those problems into good opportunities to show off your strengths. Being enthusiastic about finding solutions to problems will not only motivate you, but may motivate your boss to think more positively of you and your performance. Once you begin to switch your focus from concentrating on problems to finding solutions, you may discover that you find more solutions on a regular basis.

Suppose you have been assigned a mundane task. Not everything that goes on in an office is exciting or fun. Many details need to be taken care of that are just plain boring, such as filing, setting up for a meeting, cleaning up after a meeting, and taking food and drink orders. You probably do not want to do these minor tasks, and it can be a challenge to motivate yourself to do so. However, by doing them quickly, efficiently, and to the best of your abilities, you have the opportunity to make two things immediately clear to your employer — one, that you can be counted on get work done quickly, and two, that you likely have skills beyond what has just been asked of you. If you are able to get mundane tasks done quickly, let your boss know you are done and ready to move on to something more challenging. Your employer will likely appreciate being able to count on you and will be more keen on respecting that your talents can be better used on more complicated projects.

Suppose you have been asked to come in early or late for a project. Being tired is an excuse that people lean on to justify less-than-stellar performance. It can be a challenge to continue pushing yourself when you were counting on some time off. If you are asked to come in early or to stay late, be the employee who does so with a positive look on his or her face and a spring in his or her step. Do not complain about the hour; just do the work that is assigned.

Also, recognize that if you are coming in early or staying late, you are likely part of a smaller crew. This is a good time to get to know your fellow employees and your supervisor better. You should not do this through mindless or irrelevant small talk that distracts from the work, but through conversation that relates to what you are doing. A positive attitude, plus an active interest in what you are doing, will make you stand out from the pack and will turn the challenge of extra hours into an opportunity to make a good impression on people who will ultimately be responsible for awarding you your raise.

Suppose you have been asked to pick up the overflow for another employee. As you are reading this book, it is clear you are serious about your career. Not everyone may be as serious, and from time to time, you may be asked to help make up for deficiencies in another employee's performance. Or it may be that another employee has had an emergency or personal situation arise and is simply not able to complete a given assignment. Whatever the reason, you may be asked to do work that was not initially yours.

When you are working hard to finish your own work, it can be a challenge to take on work that someone else is not able to do. It may be tempting to complain and drag your feet to get this extra work done, but with the right attitude, you can turn this challenge into an opportunity to demonstrate that you can juggle multiple projects with ease.

Suppose a project is taking more time, energy, or resources than you had anticipated. Before taking on an assignment or project, we create expectations for how long that assignment or project should take. While we may be right much of time, we may also be off on our projections from time to time. When this happens, it can be tempting to throw up our hands and say that the project cannot be done. However, a situation like this is a perfect opportunity to spend some time speaking to your boss about potential solutions.

If you find you are not able to complete a project in a given amount of time, schedule some time with your boss to discuss the project. First, make sure you absolutely cannot finish the project in the time you originally allotted. Then, spend some time documenting exactly what you have done and what unexpected issues came up that were preventing you from finishing as you had originally planned. Come up with another projected timeline and potential solutions to the problems that arose.

Bring all of this information to your employer when you discuss needing extra time. Keep a positive attitude in the meeting. Instead of stressing the problems and what went wrong, emphasize the solutions you have developed. This attitude will be more helpful in getting you out of the situation and will show your employer that you are capable of finding solutions to problems as they arise.

CASE STUDY: MEG MCENROE

Meg McEnroe
Office manager
Los Angeles, California

"As part of an office manager position," McEnroe said, "I was often in charge of training new employees just starting to work their ways up in business. Most of my trainees were eager to prove themselves and to enter the workforce."

The most common mistakes new workers made were assuming that menial tasks are not as important as bigger, more complicated projects; speaking to co-workers and upper management too casually in their first weeks of employment; not taking punctuality seriously, even though it is perhaps one of the most important aspects of being a reliable employee; and, finally, an inability to accept constructive criticism without taking it personally.

The employees who did best were those who made real effort in all of their responsibilities and thought on their feet to solve problems without requiring direction. McEnroe said she considered them her best, most reliable employees. Most of these individuals realized that even if you have a college degree, handouts and promotions are not given without intense attention to detail and support to the team, no matter what the task is, she explained.

"I would tell any young employee to take ten-minute breaks when possible to prevent burnout while completing mundane tasks, but to also keep in mind that while it feels as though mundane tasks are insignificant, they are, in fact, stepping stones to their professional futures. I would also suggest that when they discover a more efficient way of doing something, they should approach their managers and professionally present their idea. Often, this will not only make a task less mundane, but could lead to more interesting projects directed toward them," said McEnroe.

Dress for Success

Dressing for success does not mean you have to exhaust your financial resources by buying the most expensive business attire, but it does mean you should dress as though you belong in a professional work environment. If you look like someone in a higher position than you currently hold, others in your office will start to see you that way as well.

If you deal with customers or clients, you should always dress in at least a business-casual manner. Ideally, you should have a pressed suit or nicer clothing choices available in the office, or somewhere near the office and easily accessible, in the event you must entertain unexpected clients. Your employers and those you entertain will appreciate your effort.

With that said, you should not dress out of character for your office. Many businesses are now more relaxed in what they expect their employees to wear. Casual Fridays; jeans in the office; and trendy, if not formal, clothes are quite common in many contemporary places of business. Though most offices still appreciate having their employees looking like businessmen and women, over-dressing to an extreme may cause you to look out of place instead of on your way up. You may not want to wear a suit and tie on a casual Friday when all your co-workers are wearing jeans and polo shirts.

The best way to determine how to dress is to look at the decision makers — the higher-level executives and other employees who have been recently promoted or rewarded with increases in pay or responsibility. Do they wear suits and ties, or do they arrive at work with trendy (but still well-put-together) clothing choices? For the women — do the high-ranking women in your office wear much jewelry or makeup? Are their nails done? For the men — what about facial hair? Do the executives sport a constant five o'clock shadow, or are they clean-shaven? Is their hair long or short? Making these important observations is not about mindlessly following the crowd, but about making sure that others can visualize you in the role you are working toward.

Regardless of how others in your office dress, there are some straightforward guidelines that generally will work, regardless of your place of employment.

For men:

- Pressed slacks in grey, black, or khaki
- Button-down shirts in basic colors
- Black dress socks
- Hard-soled leather shoes — no tennis shoes
- Clean-shaven faces with neat haircuts

For women:

- Pressed slacks with blouses
- Knee-length or longer skirts
- Closed-toe shoes
- Nude or sheer-colored pantyhose

There are also some hard-and-fast rules about dressing well for your look and shape. Any fashion magazine can tell men or women the better pieces of clothing for their body shape, hair color, or activity level. Looking at these types of publications can give you a good starting point toward building a wardrobe. Here are some other tips for creating an effective business wardrobe:

- **Buy two or three classic suits in different, but complementary, colors.** This will allow you to wear the pieces of each suit separately to create many different combinations that will work well in the office.

- **Sweater sets.** A sweater with a button-down, collared shirt to wear underneath will provide additional variety in your business wardrobe. You can wear the items together, separately, or with the pieces of the suits mentioned above for a classic, attractive business look.

- **Matching belts.** Belts can bring an outfit together or distract from it. Having two nice belts — one black, one brown — will keep you ready to bring any ensemble together. Make sure your belt and shoes are the same color.

- **Do not forget the socks — trouser socks should be worn under slacks.** The socks should match or complement the color of the outfit. Be careful when it comes to the temptation to "jazz up" your outfit with a colorful pair of socks. While this can look nice in the right circumstances, it can be distracting or look silly if done poorly.

It is also wise to check your company policy about tattoos and body piercings. Many companies expect employees to keep them covered during work hours.

CASE STUDY: JENARO BATIZ-ROMERO

Jenaro Batiz-Romero
Public relations
Los Angeles, California

Jenaro Batiz-Romero, who works in public relations for a political office in Los Angeles, California, explained that the dress code where he works is business-formal, which requires suits for men and women:

"It's very dressy and business-like," he said. "No jeans allowed. On Fridays, we can go business casual, which is basically the same attire, only without a tie. The business-casual wardrobe can be expensive, so you have to be creative. So I usually look for sales. Also, the big department stores usually have good deals."

"When I first started, it was like a culture shock," said Batiz-Romero. "The place I worked before was a health foods store, so the attire was very 'hippie chic:' A lot of denim and short-sleeved T-shirts and athletic shoes. So it [dressing up] felt very stuffy. But after a while, you forget about it and realize that's the name of the game and get used to it. Personally, I like it, and I like to see people dressed up. I like the elegance of business attire. Even if it is mandatory."

Wearing scents sensibly

In the right amount, perfume and cologne can accent and enhance a person's appearance, but if someone wears too much, eyes will water, noses will burn, and your pay raise will become less of a sure thing. Wearing an appropriate amount of perfume or cologne is not just about making you look — and smell — better, but can be an issue of etiquette as well.

Other scents

There are other odors that can help or harm you when it comes to your promotion. Body odor and breath can be two of the most offensive smells out there. You may become easily embarrassed when talking about body odor and breath, but you need to make sure you know exactly where you stand before moving on. Ask someone you know and trust whether your breath and body odor are normally pleasant, unnoticeable, or offensive. Let them know you need this information to help you in the workplace — and, consequently, in your personal life — and ask them to be completely honest with you. If you are too embarrassed to speak to a personal contact, visit a doctor to get an assessment of your odors. If there is a medical problem causing you to have a problem with body odor, your medical professional may prescribe a medicine to help. Assuming you are healthy, here are some tips to keep you smelling like a rose — or, at least, a higher-level employee:

- **Pack your bag.** A toiletry bag with toothpaste, toothbrush, floss, and deodorant can be a valuable asset to have on hand. Keep the bag in your car or someplace where you can easily access it during the day. After lunch, snacks, or a stressful meeting where you might have been sweating, freshen yourself up in the restroom.

- **Keep something to freshen your breath at your desk.** Mint is an obvious go-to, but if you dislike the taste or find many commercial mints too strong, citrus fruit can be used in a pinch to keep your mouth fresh. Sucking on a lemon or orange slice, or chewing a sprig of parsley, can be just as effective.

- **Do not over-swish.** Bad breath comes from bacteria in the mouth. If you use an exceedingly strong mouthwash too often, your body may retaliate by over-producing the bacteria that cause bad breath in the first place.

- **Avoid alcohol or pungent foods at the office.** Prevention is key, and one way to ensure that your breath is fresh is to eat healthy-breath food while you are at the office. These foods include fresh fruits and vegetables, clear liquids, and lean meats. Avoid eating incredibly strong-tasting foods like fish, beef, curries, onions, and peppers. The odors from strong foods not only affect your breath, but may also seep out in sweat.

- **Dress for the office, not the weather.** If it is chilly outside but warm in your office, make sure to dress in layers that you can remove inside. If you are constantly warm, you will likely sweat a little all day. Even if the sweat is not running off your forehead, it will still be there and create an odor. Dressing in layers will allow you to regulate your body temperature before your sweat glands do it for you.

- **Be your own fan — or at least bring one.** If your office is warm, invest in a small desk fan to keep yourself cool. Many offices may even have fans to lend in their operations departments.

CASE STUDY: B. CLAIRE CROUCH

B. Claire Crouch
Certified public accountant
Cosby, Tennessee

B. Claire Crouch, a retired certified public accountant who worked in Manhattan, explained that employee appearance is extremely important when asking for a pay raise or advancement within a company.

"When meeting about a pay raise or advancement, appearance is important," she said. "The employee should look well-groomed, organized, and professional."

Crouch said some of the mistakes an employee should avoid include coming to the meeting unprepared, looking sloppy, or getting emotional during the meeting. She also pointed out that wearing strong scents, such as too much cologne or perfume, are major mistakes. Strong organizational skills are vital in proving your point, she added.

In addition, Crouch said the employee should be able to have a "well-thought-out discussion about their contributions to the company and why he or she deserves a raise."

Body language can show confidence, assurance, and poise — or the lack thereof — during the meeting. Employees should be able to show they have met goals, budgets, and quotas, as well as improved performance, she said.

If business is doing well, Crouch believes an employee who does well and improves their value to the employer should request a pay raise annually.

When giving pay raises or considering promotions, she explained that supervisors consider several factors, including the employee's value to the company; the employee's goals and how they mesh with the company's goals; ways the employee has improved; and any new skills he or she has learned, as well as whether the employee is a team player and a self-starter who has brought new ideas to the company.

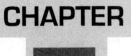

CHAPTER 7

Communication

There are many levels to communication, and it is imperative that a business professional master all of them. In business, you deal with people on the phone, over e-mail, through physical correspondence, and face-to-face. Each of these modes of communication requires an understanding of how to do them effectively.

Face-to-Face Verbal Communication

You will spend considerable time talking to people to do your job. Making sure you do so correctly and professionally will ensure that your communication is effective. The more effective you make your communication, the easier it will be for you to explain why you deserve a pay raise — and to earn it.

Meetings

Meetings come in all shapes and sizes — from one-on-one meetings to speaking in front of large groups. You may be called upon to present information to various audiences, and you need to learn to conduct yourself to ensure maximum impact.

One-on-one

You will speak differently in a small, intimate meeting with just another or a handful of participants. In this kind of a meeting, you are free to start with small talk and friendly pleasantries. You may want to ask how people are doing. If you are aware of personal yet safe information, you may want to ask questions about those topics to lighten the mood. For example, if one of the participants has recently moved to a new floor at the office, ask how the move is going or whether they need any help. Though this is a time to be friendly, avoid personal information. You are there to discuss business, and personal issues should be kept out of the office.

After you have taken a minute to establish rapport, quickly move into the purpose of the meeting. Everyone's time is valuable. While the group will appreciate your politeness, they will also want to move on to the meeting's focus. Do not keep them waiting.

Group meetings or presentations

If you are giving a report or presenting information to a large group of people, you will need to keep the attention focused on you. This is not the time to make small talk before the meeting starts. Instead, start by welcoming everyone to the meeting and letting them know the topic of discussion.

Make everyone at the meeting feel included. Speak clearly, slowly, and loudly so everyone in the room can hear you. If you are using a microphone, check the level of the sound before the meeting starts so you do not take up time fixing a technical glitch. Making regular eye contact with everyone in the room is essential to ensure no one is left out of the discussion.

If you are not in charge of the meeting but are simply a participant, do not let that stop you from being involved. Take care to note the hierarchy. If this is not a meeting where your input is needed, do not insert yourself just to get attention. Listen attentively and make eye contact with the speaker. Nod your head and use body language to confer you are paying attention to the topic and are interested in what is being discussed. When a senior executive is talking, make eye contact with him or her to show that you are actively listening.

If you have something to add to the discussion, make sure it pertains to the topic of discussion. A group meeting is not the time to bring up topics that are only tangentially related. Make your statement or question clear and concise. Speak only when it is your turn or when you are asked for your input.

One way to make your comments stand out — and to make sure they stay on-point — is to say things like: "In addition to what Melissa just said…" Statements like this show that you are listening and not just trying to get your voice heard. These kinds of comments also bring more people into the conversation. Using people's names is a powerful way to get their attention and keep it. The person to whom you referred will appreciate your validating their comment.

CASE STUDY: JOSHUA LOYD

Joshua Loyd
Retail manager
Newport, Tennessee

Joshua Loyd, a retail manager, says he expects an employee to show self-confidence when requesting a pay raise. "Poor posture, slouching, and so forth show a lack of confidence and a lack of belief that the employee really deserves the raise they are asking for," he said.

Loyd believes going beyond the company's expectations and performing above average can earn a pay raise for an employee, and he feels that pay raises and advancement should be solely based on ability to perform. "However, dress is often taken highly into consideration. If one does not look the 'part,' often it seems as if managers feel as if they will not be able to perform the job," he added.

When asking for a pay raise, "The best documentation is showing or displaying what the employee has done to better the company or firm. Also: Reports from that employee's specific department that display above-average returns or profits, and statements showing how the employee asking for the raise significantly impacted the above-average numbers," he says.

When is the right time to ask for a pay raise? Loyd says several factors should be considered: "How is your boss's mood? How is the company/division/store performing?"

General meeting guidelines

Regardless of the size of the meeting, there are some general guidelines you should follow. These guidelines will help you accomplish what needs to be taken care of, and will also make you stand out as a capable communicator, which will put you in a stronger position to receive your pay raise.

- **Have an agenda.** You should know exactly what needs to be discussed at your meeting and what you hope to accomplish. Print your agenda, and give a copy to the meeting participants. This will keep everyone on the same page and prevent the conversation from straying.

- **Stick to a schedule.** Keep an eye on the clock, and make sure your meeting is not running long. This is not only polite, but it will keep things moving and ensure that work is done efficiently.

- **Summarize.** At the beginning of the meeting, let the participants know what you will be discussing. This will focus everyone's attention on what needs to be done. At the end of the meeting, you should also summarize key points. This will give everyone the chance to correct any miscommunication. It will also ensure that the important parts of what was discussed stay in the minds of the participants.

- **Leave time for questions.** You will want to give the meeting participants a chance to ask questions. Make sure there is some time at the end of your meeting to explain anything that was unclear.

- **Listen actively.** With the stress of making sure a meeting goes the way it is supposed to, it can be easy to relax when others are talking, but take care to listen actively. This involves maintaining eye contact, using positive body language, and asking questions that show you are listening.

- **Treat all participants with respect.** Regardless of where you are in the hierarchy of the company, or where anyone else in the meeting is, you should treat everyone with the highest level of respect. All opinions are valid, and everyone deserves to be heard. Address people by their proper titles, and do not talk down to employees whom you outrank.

The Phone

Next to face-to-face conversations, the telephone should be your primary source of business communication. Even though e-mail is quick and easy, valuable aspects of communication are lost when you cannot hear another person's voice. Inflection plays a huge part in setting tone; with e-mails, since inflection is lost, the tone of your e-mail may not arrive as you intended.

Even when using the phone, some aspects of communication are lost because you are not making eye contact or observing body language or facial expressions. Therefore, it is important to fine-tune other communication skills; that way, your message is received clearly and effectively. Next, we will examine the various parts of a phone conversation and how to maximize the effectiveness of each.

The greeting

Your greeting should be clear and easily understood. In a business setting, it is not enough to answer your phone with "Hello." If you are receiving calls from outside your office, you should state the company name and your name to assure the caller that he or she has reached the correct phone number. Your greeting should sound something like this: "Good afternoon. Thank you for calling 'The Company.' This is 'Jane Doe.' How can I help you?" Although it may sound wordy, it will assure anyone calling who you are and that you can help them. The more comfortable your company's clients are with you, the easier it will be to prove that you deserve a pay raise.

If you are fielding calls from inside your office, you should state your name and department. For example: "Operations, this is John Doe." Or "Operations, John Doe speaking." This allows the caller to immediately know whether they have called the correct department, and it will give the caller a sense of comfort to know immediately who you are.

Many companies have caller ID installed on their office phones. Knowing who is calling may tempt you to answer with a simple "Hello?" — especially if you know the person well. But there are a few things to remember about defaulting to a casual answer that should prevent you from doing so:

- Someone else may be calling from your friend's phone.

- Your friend may be on a tight deadline, and therefore, not in a chatty mood.

- A higher-level employee or executive may be passing by and may not appreciate hearing such a casual greeting on what they will assume is a business call.

If you are the one making the call, then when the phone is answered, identify yourself and the person you are calling. For example: "Hello, this is John Doe. Is Jane Doe available?" It is fine to make polite conversation with the person who answers the phone — especially if this is a contact you will be calling often — but keep it brief, and quickly get to the point of your phone call. This will maintain your professional appearance to the person answering the phone and will ensure that you are able to conduct your business in a timely manner.

If you are calling a contact who knows you, resist the urge to simply say, "Hey, Jane. It is John." While this may work for a contact you know well, it is dangerous territory for a contact with whom you have a comfortable, yet casual relationship. A higher-ranking employee may not appreciate your casual approach to him or her on the phone. Instead, if your contact is a higher-ranking employee, you should say, "Hello, Mr. Johnson, this is Jane Doe. Do you have a minute to discuss the print schedule?" A greeting like this lets your contact know that you are calling with a purpose, are ready to discuss that purpose, and you respect their position and time.

If you are calling a contact with whom you have a close personal relationship, it is fine to use a more casual greeting. Yet, you should move quickly into the reason for the call. This will allow anyone within earshot — including executives who may control your raise — to know that when you get on the phone, you are doing it to accomplish business, and not simply to pass the time or to make personal conversation.

The conversation

The biggest issue to guard against when talking on the phone is distraction. Without someone sitting across from you and looking you in the eye, it will be easy to be distracted by items on your desk, other people in your office, people outside the window, or your computer screen. Allowing yourself to be distracted will hurt your chances at communicating effectively on the phone.

The first part of communicating well on the phone, then, is to minimize distractions. If you work in your own office, shut the door before beginning a phone call. If you receive an important phone call while your office door is open, ask the caller whether you may put them on hold for just a second to shut the door, so you can ensure privacy as well as your undivided attention.

If you work in a cubicle or at an open-air desk, having privacy and freeing yourself from distractions may be more difficult, but it is possible. Sit so you are facing away from both the main flow of traffic and away from your computer screen. This will prevent you from being distracted by people walking by or from anything on your computer screen. If your back is facing the main flow of traffic, this will also clue others in to the fact that you are on an important call and should not be disturbed.

When doing business on the phone, you should have any important paperwork or documents that you need in easy reach. This will prevent you from having to hunt for information while you are on the phone. It will also allow you to quickly answer any questions your contact may have or to be able to ask your contact any questions you may need answered.

When you have a conversation on the phone, as with e-mail, you lose much in the way of communication. You miss out on non-verbal cues such as facial expression and body language. Because of this, you will need to be careful that you do not miss crucial parts of your conversations. Here are some tips to make sure that your phone conversations are as efficient and effective as possible:

- **Slow down.** Though technology has made phone lines incredibly clear, static and noise on the line is not a thing of the past. Because your contact is not in front of you to read your lips, you will need to slow your speech down a bit to make sure they have the chance to catch every word.

- **Ask leading questions.** Instead of asking questions like, "Do you like this idea?" ask leading questions, like, "What do you think of this idea?" Asking questions that illicit a "yes" or "no" answer may make it easier for your contact to answer less thoughtfully. Because you are not making eye contact, it will be easier to miss clues that would let you know how your contact feels about your question. Instead, ask open-ended questions, which allow your contact to answer more fully. A more complete answer from your contact will make up for the lack of non-verbal clues.

- **Reword and repeat.** Restating what your phone contact has said will give you the opportunity to make sure you heard him or her correctly, and him or her the chance to correct you if you did not. It also indicates that you are paying attention. Because you are on the phone, you do not have the benefit of nods or shaking heads to clue you into agreement or disagreement from your contact. Repeating what you heard back to them will take the place of those non-verbal actions.

- **Record.** Recording your phone conversation will allow you to listen and speak without having to worry about making notes at the same time. There are easy-to-use devices that can be purchased from office supply stores or small electronics stores that you can use to record phone conversations as they are happening. These devices are excellent tools to use to make sure you do not miss any part of the conversation. When you are done with the phone call, you have the option to transcribe the conversation or simply review sections of it as you need to. Label and file the tapes so that you can find them again easily. You do also need to make sure your contact is aware that the conversation is being recorded.

- **Take notes.** If you do need to take notes, and cannot get by with recording the phone call to be transcribed later, take notes efficiently. If you are an expert typist and can type more than 60 words a minute, you may be able to nearly transcribe your conversation as it happens, word by word. If your typing skills are not as fast, you may feel more comfortable making handwritten notes.

- **Stay organized.** Keep your pens or pencils handy so you do not get distracted looking for new ones should you need them. Try to make notes on the materials you have collected for the meeting so that you do not have to shuffle the meeting materials and your note-taking materials as well. Keeping track of so many pieces of paper may cause you to lose them or to get distracted, missing out on important information. When you are done with your meeting, review your notes with your phone contact so you are sure they are clear and accurate.

The closing

The way you end a phone conversation is just as important as the way you begin it. You want to leave your phone contact with the confidence and reassurance that your phone call was effective and mutually beneficial. You also want to leave them knowing that they can count on you to communicate on the phone in the future.

When ending a phone conversation, you should first review any pertinent information. Go over your notes one more time to see whether you have any lingering questions. Ask whether there was anything they felt was left out or any items they would like to follow up on. If there are things they wish to follow up on, ask them when they would like to do the follow-up. Reconfirm any new information you receive at the conversation's conclusion.

The ending salutation should be professional and polite. It will also be effective to leave the conversation with both parties knowing that you will speak again — especially if you are talking to a higher-ranking employee. You should say something like, "Thank you for your time, Mr. Johnson. I will send you the notes by the end of the day and address the items we discussed by the end of the week." Of course, you do not want to give yourself a schedule you cannot follow through with, but you should work to resolve any issues you discussed in your conversation as quickly as possible.

The outgoing message

Your outgoing message is what people will hear when you are not able to answer the phone. It should be brief and clear. People will want to know that they have reached the correct extension or phone number.

Your outgoing message should go something like, "Hello, you have reached John Doe in human resources. Please leave me a message, and I will return your call as soon as I am able." Because we have all heard so many outgoing messages, you may be tempted to jazz up your outgoing message with humor or a joke. While that may be fine for your home phone, it will not sound professional to others calling your office. A straightforward outgoing message is the best way to go.

If you are comfortable doing so, you may choose to leave an alternative phone number at which a caller may reach you. This is helpful if you are regularly away from your desk or phone. If you leave an alternative phone number, say the number slowly and repeat it so that callers do not have to call back to get the information. For example: "Hello, you have reached John Doe in human resources. Please leave me a message, and I will return your call as soon as I am able. If this is an urgent matter, you may reach me at 310-555-1212. Again, if this is urgent, you may contact me at 310-555-1212." Be aware that people will likely take advantage of an alternative number, so do not give out that information if you do not intend to use it.

Sometimes, you will be away from your office for an extended period of time. If that is the case, it will be helpful to leave information for another person whom a caller may contact if their call is urgent. For example: "Hello, you have reached John Doe in human resources. I will be out of the office until Monday, May 18. If you need assistance before then, contact Julia Michaels at 310-

555-1213. That contact again is Julia Michaels at 310-555-1213."
Do not volunteer someone to be your alternative contact. Speak
with him or her beforehand and find out whether he or she is able
to handle your phone calls while you are out of the office.

Leaving a voicemail

When you leave a voicemail, try to convey as much information
as possible, and as efficiently as possible. Do not leave long, rambling messages that meander around a point. Instead, mention
the bullet points of the conversation and a time in which you
would like to receive a return call.

For example: "Hello, Rich. This is April Summers from production. I wanted to talk to you about extending the deadline for
the Sanchez report. If my office had two more days to complete
it, we would be able to finalize some numbers. Please let me
know by the end of the day whether this will be possible. You
can reach me at extension 1214. Again, you can reach me at
extension 1214. Thank you."

Be polite and to the point. Giving as much information as possible will allow the person you are calling to prepare any necessary information before calling you back. This will streamline the
work that needs to be done and prevent any unnecessary back-
and-forth calling.

Physical Correspondence: Letters, Faxes, E-mail, and Memos

Though much business correspondence is done via e-mail, a
good part of business is still done traditionally with letters and

faxes. It is imperative, then, to understand how to correctly format and effectively write business letters and faxes. Good letter writing will help you stand out from the pack and be in a stronger position to get your raise. In addition, you may be writing your employer to request a raise, and you want to be able to craft the best letter possible.

Many people make the mistake of thinking that because they write often, they write well. And some people may think that because they are used to speaking and using the language, they must be able to write effectively. Writing well is a craft of its own, and care should be taken to make sure your writing is as effective and as clear as possible.

Every detail matters when writing — from proper formatting, to organization, to word choice. In the following sections, we will discuss all of these aspects so your business writing helps you get closer to earning your raise.

Formatting a business letter

Header

Business letter writing begins with a header. The header lets the reader know who wrote the letter, the date the letter was written, and to whom the letter is being sent. Much like your greeting to start a phone call, the letter's header is designed to deliver a large amount of information quickly. The following is an example of a business letter's header:

Jane Fawn
Manager, Human Resources
Company of Today
12345 Main St.
Cityville, ST 10001

March 15, 2008

Mr. John Doe
Vice President, Marketing
Company of Tomorrow
54321 Main St.
Cityville, ST 10001

Dear Mr. Doe:

Let us look at each part of this header. Understanding the purpose of each part of the header will make it easier for you to remember what goes where. And the more quickly you are able to recall this information, the more quickly you will be able to efficiently produce business correspondence.

The first part of the header lets the recipient know who sent the letter. The header should begin with the sender's name. Underneath the header comes the sender's title company and the company's address. In addition to making it clear from whom the letter is coming, it also makes it easy for the recipient to return the correspondence by putting the contact information in a place that is easy to find.

Finally, the date appears. The date allows the recipient to prioritize his or her response. Putting the date in the header allows the reader to know when the letter was sent and to arrange a date by which to respond to the letter. It also protects the reader from being told that something was sent before it was — and protects the sender from being told that something was sent after it was. A proper header should have the recipient's name followed by title, then company, and then company address. It may seem like excessive information, but it is crucial that company and business information be exchanged only between the parties involved.

If you are writing a letter on company letterhead, the contact information of the sender may already be in place. If this is the case, you will be able to skip the first half of the heading and start with the date and the recipient's address. You should check to see whether the letterhead gives specific information about the sender, or simply about the company itself. If it is not personalized stationery, you should include the sender's information so it is clear who the letter is coming from.

Next is the salutation. This is where you address the person to whom you have sent the letter. It consists of just a few words at most, but with the right salutation, you send the message that you are respectful and professional.

You should always try to have an exact person to address in the salutation. Try to avoid "Dear Sirs," "Dear Sir or Madam," or "To Whom it May Concern." They may have a ring of professionalism, but you will make a much stronger connection if you address someone directly. Generic salutations like those just mentioned may inadvertently make it look as though you are simply not interested in taking the time to find out to whom you need to be speaking.

If you are sending a piece of correspondence on behalf of someone else, that person will likely provide you with the proper name. Be sure to check the spelling of the name. You can do this by calling the contact's office. Avoid simply relying on a company contact list, as there may be errors on that document.

When you have your contact's name, the salutation should follow the pattern of: "Dear Mr. Johnson," or "Dear Dr. Sanchez." "Dear" is a standard greeting and is accepted throughout business. The person should be addressed with "Mr." or "Ms." followed by his or her last name. If the person has a title in which he or she is commonly addressed — such as "Dr." — then that title should be used instead of "Mr." or "Ms."

In the case of ambiguous names, you should unquestionably make sure you are addressing your letter to a person of the correct gender. While it may be embarrassing to ask for this information, it will be more embarrassing to call Ms. Alex Summers "Mr. Alex Summers." Here are some tips for solving the mystery of a name that could belong to either a man or a woman:

- If the person is in your office building, walk by his or her office. This will not only solve the mystery of their gender, but also give you the chance to make a face-to-face contact.

- Check in with your human resources department with a visit or phone call, and pose your problem something like this: "I need to send a letter to Alex Summers. I have never met Alex Summers, and I mean no offense by asking, but should I address this to Mr. or Ms. Summers?"

- Call his or her office to get the correct spelling of his or her name. If the contact answers the call, you will be able to hear his or her voice and have your answer. If his or her assistant answers, you will be able to check the spelling and ascertain how you should address your letter.

Body

The name of the game, when it comes to crafting the body of your letter, is organization. The letter should be as brief as possible, while still being clear. The way to do this is to make sure your paragraphs are organized.

The opening paragraph should explain what the purpose of the correspondence is; each following paragraph should support your reason for writing, and your final paragraph should summarize what you have discussed in the letter.

Each paragraph should start with a topic sentence. This sentence should make it clear what the rest of the paragraph will be about. Each following sentence should support the topic sentence. Your paragraphs should be at least three sentences long, and the final sentence should offer a sense of summary or conclusion to the sentences that came before it.

Here is an example of a well-crafted paragraph. Let us say that this is the first paragraph of the letter. See whether you can identify the parts of the paragraph, as described above.

> The Thompson account is experiencing an unexpected delay. Though our office invoiced for the work completed thus far, the client has not paid in full. Without their next payment, my office is not comfortable proceeding with the project, as the work is very time-intensive. We are looking to rectify this situation as soon as possible, and we wanted to make you aware of the situation.

This paragraph gets right to the point. Even though the news is not good news, there is no beating around the bush. Instead, the letter dives right into the issue. This facilitates clarity and ease of understanding. While you may be tempted to massage bad news, your contact will likely appreciate sticking to the point at-hand and getting to the point quickly.

When it comes to format, there are a few things to note. It is accepted to either indent the first line or to leave it flush with the margin. Either way, each paragraph should have a blank line between it and the next paragraph. You should also leave a space between a period at the end of a sentence and the following sentence. Proper formatting makes your letter easy to read and makes you look professional.

Another way to make your correspondence simple to read is to use bullets in the context of your letter. Bullets are a quick way to draw the reader's eye to important information. Most word processing programs have bullets included in their formatting options, so not only are they easy to read, but they are easy to use. Here is an example of a paragraph that uses bullets:

My office understands that a physical move of our staff would be a large undertaking. However, a move would allow us to more effectively complete upcoming projects. There are several reasons why a move would be the best thing for my staff at this time:

- Several projects require that we run multiple printers simultaneously. A larger space would allow us to install enough printers to complete our work efficiently.

- More offices would allow our clients to feel more comfortable having private conversations and creative meetings with our representatives.

- Extra cubicle space would allow us to make room for another assistant to handle overflow that our executives do not have time to complete themselves.

The bullets in the preceding section make quick work of a long list of justifications for more office space. This kind of presentation would allow the recipient to easily make the case to their supervisor to honor the writer's request. Efficiency and clarity are paramount in business communication, and bullets make things exceptionally clear.

You should also pay attention to sentence structure. Simple sentences are best and will provide maximum clarity. Avoid long, rambling, or run-on sentences that may confuse your reader. A good way to determine whether your sentences are too long is to highlight sentences in alternating colors. If you find that any of your sentences goes on for more than two lines, you should revise that sentence to make it shorter and simpler.

Your letter should also be free from spelling and grammar mistakes. A careless mistake in word choice, spelling, or syntax will ruin the effectiveness of your letter. Review your letter for these kinds of mistakes. If you are unsure whether a word is the correct one to use or whether a sentence was formatted correctly, revise the sentence using vocabulary and structure that you are more comfortable with. It is better to be simple and clear with your message than to try to sound high society and miss the mark.

Closing

When it comes to ending your letter, your ending salutation should be friendly and professional. A simple "Best Regards," or "Sincerely," will work well. Though it is often used, "Thank You," is not a proper closing salutation. While you should thank your contact for taking the time to read your letter, you should include that sentiment in the closing paragraph.

Your name comes next. After the closing salutation, insert a comma and hit the return key four times to create three blank lines between the salutation and your typed name. The space allows room for you to sign your name to the letter.

Finally, there are several abbreviations that come after your signature and typed name. These abbreviations, explained below, provide a final round of important information for your reader.

- **Enc.** — This abbreviation stands for "Enclosure." It lets the reader know that there is more to what was sent than the letter that they are reading. It is best to include information about any enclosures in the body of your letter. This abbreviation reminds the reader to look for other material that was sent.

- **CC** — This lets the reader know another person has an exact copy of what was sent to your contact. The other recipient did not receive their own personalized copy, but simply a carbon copy of what the reader has. This gives the reader the chance to know who else has the information that he or she is privy to in case he or she has questions or wishes to discuss the information with others in his or her office.

- **/abc** — If someone transcribed your letter, this abbreviation lets the reader know who did the transcription. The three letters stand for the initials of the person who did the transcription. This not only lets the reader know who else knows about the information in the letter, it also provides a person to go to if there is a mistake in the letter. Therefore, if it is you, make sure your letter is free from typos.

Finishing up your letter

Before you send your letter, take a few precautions to make sure it is in the best shape that it can be in. A typo, wrong name, or unclear sentence can sabotage your letter. Here are the things you will need to do before you send off your letter:

- **Spell check.** Most word processing programs have their own spell-check programs. Run it, but do not rely on it. There are nuances to the language that automated programs do not catch. You also run the risk of "correcting" a word that the computer sees as misspelled that is actually correct.

- **Print your letter out and read it from the page — not just from the computer screen.** You may catch typos you missed before when you look at your letter from a different perspective.

- **Fact check.** Go through your letter, and if there is any factual information, check each fact individually. This will ensure total accuracy in your letter. If there are company facts and figures involved, check them with an objective party, such as company documents or another department.

- **Make it pretty.** Print out your letter and make sure all the elements look good on the page. The letter should be centered on the page, with not too much space on the top or the bottom. Likewise, the text should only be about an inch from either side of the page. Any more than that and the text will look too crunched. Less than that, and the page will look too crowded.

- **The font should be one that is easy to read.** Book Antiqua and Times New Roman are good all-purpose fonts that are easy to read. Your text should be between 10 and 12-point font. Smaller than that, and your letter will be difficult to read. Larger than that, and not only will it be difficult to read, it will be reminiscent of college papers that are short on substance, but large on font.

Faxes

A letter that is being faxed should be formatted exactly as a business letter that is being sent through the mail. There are a few differences between a fax and a letter that you should be aware of to ensure your paperwork arrives clearly and without questions. These differences have to do with the way a fax is sent and received.

Every faxed letter should be preceded by a cover page. This page should give not only the company information, but information about the fax. You include the number of pages — including the title page — that are being sent. In other words, if you are sending a three-page letter, plus a cover page, you should indicate on the cover page that you are faxing four pages. This will ensure that your recipient receives all the pages that were faxed. You should also include your own fax number so that your contact can easily return your fax.

The quality of fax machines varies significantly, and your correspondence should be formatted in a way that allows for this variation. The document should be printed with dark ink and a clear font. This will prevent the fax from losing part of the text as it copies or blurring together parts of your document. Any information that is highlighted in your original copy should be underlined or boxed in the fax. A fax machine will not be able to read the relatively slight variation in color from a highlighter, or it may read the highlighted section as one dark bar. As with a letter, review your document before sending so it is as clear as possible.

It is always a good idea to call and make sure your fax arrived at its destination. Between the potential for jammed phone lines, other employees accidentally picking up your fax by mistake, or even an empty paper tray or ink cartridge, it is relatively easy for a fax to be missed by your contact. When you call, let them know the time the fax was sent and how many pages should have arrived. This will ensure your document arrives as it was intended.

E-mail

E-mail has allowed business communication to become more casual, but that does not mean your e-mails should reflect this casual attitude. A well-written e-mail, with the proper formatting and salutations, can be just as powerful as a hand-delivered letter. Also, if you keep your e-mails to higher standards, they will stand out from the pack and put you in a better light to receive your raise.

You can do without the headers in an e-mail. Because an e-mail address is so specific, you can begin your letter with "Dear Mr. Doe."

Memos

A memo is less formal than a letter and is frequently sent to many employees at once. Memos are used to distribute broad information, such as contact lists, meeting notes, and information on upcoming company events. Nonetheless, it is important that memos be treated with the same respect as business letters. The fact that so many people will see your memo means more people will be able to form opinions about your acumen as a business professional. Make sure you put your best foot forward when sending one out.

The proper format for a memo is simple. Memos are almost always distributed within a company. An example of a memo:

To:
From:
Subject:
Text of memo:

Vocabulary and Vernacular

People are judged by their use of language. Your employers will be listening to you to see whether the way you talk reflects the image they have of their team, company, and business. Make sure that when you speak, you are representing yourself well. You could be rewarded for choosing the right words with a raise.

The first thing to do to raise the level of your speech is to make sure you are using basic grammar correctly. We all had to take English classes in school, but it is easy to forget some of the lessons we learned there. Basic grammar is essential to communicating well and to proving that you are a vital part of the company. Following is an explanation of common grammar mistakes and how to correct them. Some of the mistakes come from words sounding the same (homophones), some come from confusing grammar rules, and some come from the fact that after high school, people tend to stop studying grammar in earnest. It is not necessary to get a degree in English. Simply review this list for a quick primer.

- "A lot" is two words. "Alot" is incorrect.

- "Already" is one word with one "l." "Allready" is incorrect. "All ready" can be used when done properly. Example: "We have already received the package." As an example for when all ready is correct: "They were all ready when we got there."

- Clichés and fad-speak do not make your letters and conversations sound more sophisticated. Instead, they can make what you say sound trite, sometimes even forced. Every business has words that are unique to it, but phrases like "thinking outside the box," "win-win situation," and "synergy" have lost any real meaning they once had through overuse. When speaking and writing, say what you mean without resorting to clichés, and your words will have a stronger impact.

- "I" and "me" — When referring to yourself, make sure to use the correct pronoun. "I" is used as the subject of a sentence, and "me" is used as an object. In other words "I" indicates that the speaker is doing something, and "me" indicates that something is being done to or for the speaker.

  - Correct: "Mr. Sanchez and I need to speak with you."

  - Correct: "She wants to speak to me."

  - Correct: "Stephanie gave the report to Mr. Sanchez and me."

- "Irregardless" is not the correct word. "Regardless" is correct.

- "It's" and "Its" — "It's" with the apostrophe is the contraction form of "it is." "Its" without the apostrophe is the possessive form of "it."

  - Correct: "It's time for our annual company picnic. This year, we will look at its effectiveness in teambuilding."

    - In this sentence, the first "it's" is short for "it is time for our annual company picnic." The second "its" refers to the picnic.

- Misplaced modifiers — Sometimes, adjectives find themselves far away from the words they describe, which can cause confusion.

  - Incorrect: "The meeting will cover employee lunches on Tuesday."

  - Correct: "The meeting Tuesday will cover employee lunches."

In the first sentence, it is unclear whether the meeting is on Tuesday or whether the employee lunches are on Tuesday. Keep words and phrases near the subjects they are describing.

- "They're," "their," and "there" — "They're" is a contraction and means "they are." "Their" is the possessive form of "they." "There" is an adjective or adverb.

    - Correct: "They're going to make sure that their reports are there for the meeting."

- "Too" and "to" — "Too" means also or in addition to. "To" can either be part of a verb phrase or a direction.

    - Correct: "We need to make sure that this gets to Mr. Richards, and that he gets this, too."

        - "To make" is an infinitive verb phrase, so the two-letter "to" is correct.

        - "To Mr. Richards" is a preposition, and so the two-letter "to" is correct.

        - "…gets this, too" could be written "gets this also," and so the three-letter "too" is correct.

- "Who's" and "whose" — This is another set of words that gets mixed up, like "its" and "it's" — and for similar reasons. "Who's" is a contraction and means "who is;" "Whose" shows possession.

    - Correct: "Who's going to make sure that we will know whose responsibility it is to make sure schedules are written on time?"

In terms of impressing the higher-ups, after good grammar comes a good vocabulary. A good vocabulary is crucial in showing that you know how to communicate. It is not about using big words just to use them, but about using creative, descriptive words to make sure your point gets across. A good vocabulary will also help illustrate your ideas and thoughts in a way that brings them to life for your coworkers and employers.

Increasing and/or improving your vocabulary is easier than you might think. You do not have to go back to school or invest in expensive training materials. The following are some easy ways to incorporate new words into your daily routine:

- Read newspapers and national magazines. You can decipher the meaning of many of the words you do not know from their context. Otherwise, look them up in a dictionary.

- When writing a report, memo, or letter, select a few words to try to change. Look these words up in a thesaurus and begin using their synonyms.

- Watch movies, television shows, and news reports you do not normally watch. Challenge yourself to watch and digest the information presented in these media. Doing so will not only increase your vocabulary, but your frame of reference as well.

Mastering the vernacular

Every business has its own set of words and phrases that are unique to that business. Doctors have a slew of medical terminology. Attorneys have words that reflect their legal background. Teachers will even discuss common events differently than a businessperson, architect, or flight attendant will. The type of vocabulary unique to a sub-population of people is called a vernacular. You need to be on top of your business's way of speaking.

Your employers would expect you to be able to follow along in any executive-level meeting or phone call. Your supervisor will expect you to address them with terms and a frame of reference that clearly show that you understand the business in which you are employed. Before asking for your raise, you will need to demonstrate through your vernacular that you can discuss your business intelligently.

Here are some ways to increase your knowledge and understanding of your business's vernacular:

- Read all company publications, e-mail, newsletters, and documents that you can. This will not only help you stay abreast of what is going on in your office, but you will pick up the pattern of speech and vocabulary unique to your business.

- Read trade publications. This will help you get a better understanding of your business at large. You will most likely be able to find many of these publications through your company. Otherwise, visit a library or use an online search engine.

- Speak with as many other employees and professionals in your industry as you can. This will give you real-life demonstrations on how professionals in your industry speak to each other.

Though a rich vocabulary will make you stand out as an employee, do not be tempted to use alternate words just for the sake of it. For example, if you are writing a letter about last quarter's profits, there is no need to find a different way of saying the word "profit" each time it comes up in the letter, though it may come up several times. Above all else, business communication needs to be clear and easily read. Business people are busy and will want to get whatever information they need as quickly and efficiently as possible. Cluttering your letter with unnecessary synonyms will cause your letter to lose its effectiveness and will cause you to lose the recipient's attention.

CHAPTER 8

Keep a Positive Attitude

Enjoy Working Hard

Thinking of your work simply as a series of duties that must be done can be draining and may make it difficult to see tasks through to completion. If you do not find a passion for what you are doing, you may burn yourself out before you reach your goals. Learn to enjoy the work for what it is, and you will have an easier time climbing the corporate ladder.

It can be difficult to find joy in alphabetizing files or making copies, but you can learn to look at the joy in the small picture, and the encouragement of the overall picture. Keeping your eye on both ends of the spectrum will help you take more pleasure and pride in your days at the office.

There is merit in the small things that must go on to make an office run smoothly. Filing keeps things in order. Copying material for meetings and making well-put-together presentation packets create a pleasing aesthetic in the meeting room. Taking a lunch order makes hungry executives happy. You will be able to keep a more positive attitude if you can keep these items in mind as you do the less-than-glamorous tasks that every office needs to have done.

You should also realize that such little things will get you closer to your ultimate goals — a raise and professional success. When you show that you can be counted on to take care of small tasks, it will be more likely that your boss will trust you with more. You cannot be trusted with more money and a more prestigious position at a company before you demonstrate that you can regularly meet — and exceed — what they currently expect.

Your boss will also appreciate seeing you work hard, and you should take pleasure in seeing your employer pleased with your performance. Your employer does not want to see his or her money — in this case, your salary — wasted. If you are not working hard, your employer may think that he or she has not made a good investment in you as an employee. Your employer will be even more pleased to see that you enjoy doing the work that you have been hired to do. And when your employer is pleased, you will likely be pleased at what results from his or her appreciation of your work.

Humility Looks Good on You

As you pursue your professional goals, it may feel like you need to be assertive and aggressive at all times. Though you want to show that you are confident in your work, you should remember that you always have something to learn. There will always be people who know more than you; you can always do better work. You should strive to keep a humble attitude at the office. Do not be afraid to ask for help. Respect that your boss probably knows more than you, and do not be ashamed to ask questions. A humble attitude is a positive addition to your professional persona.

Being humble involves several attitude adjustments. First, you must be honest about yourself and your work. This does not mean being overly critical of your abilities. You should take an honest look at what you do well and at any areas in which you may need more help, assistance, or direction.

When you determine what you may need help with, show that you respect your employer's expertise enough to speak with him or her about the best way to address those problems. Understanding that your boss may be able to help with your concerns about your work is another component of being humble. Present this subject to your boss with a positive attitude. Try approaching your boss with something like this: "I am worried that my annual reports are not as clear as they could be. If you do not mind, I would like to go over my recent reports with you to determine what I can do to make them stronger." In this statement, you have identified an issue without being overly critical of your work, shown that you are interested in finding a solution, and shown respect for your boss's position and experience.

Finally, you will need to demonstrate sincerity when you deal with your employers and co-workers. If you are faking your respect for your boss and fellow employees, it will show. False respect can make you look not only insincere, but arrogant as well. You definitely do not want your co-workers to get the idea that you think you are better than they are.

As we discussed earlier, regardless of your positive attitude, others may simply not warm to you for reasons you may not understand. By the same token, you may also have a hard time warming to others in your office. There may be someone — even your boss — who just rubs you the wrong way. Even in this situation, you must find a way to genuinely respect them. Consider the fact that you are all in the same boat, and let that drive your compassion and empathy for them. You all work for the same company, and if one employee experiences success, that success may be passed on to the whole team.

Likewise, if things are difficult for one part of the team, the whole team may suffer. Understanding that you are all part of one whole can help you find a way to respect, and maybe even like, difficult co-workers. Once you are able to genuinely respect your co-workers, everyone involved will appreciate your positive attitude and respect, and in turn, they will give you more respect as well.

Let Go of the Past and Start Again

Regardless of what has happened up to this point in your career or at your office, let go of any anger, frustration, doubt, worry, or bitterness that may be holding you back. It is possible that you may have good reason to be angry at a co-worker, boss, or company. However, holding on to that anger will not hurt anyone but you. If you are serious about moving forward with your career, you need to let go of the past so you can concentrate on the future.

If you have a long-standing conflict or concern with a fellow employee, schedule some time to speak to that employee to work out the issue. It may feel intimidating to have this meeting, but it is crucial you work through these problems so you can move forward. It is possible the problem was the result of a misunderstanding, or maybe the two of you just have a different way of approaching situations. Let the person know you are apologetic for your part in the problem and that you would like to find a way the two of you can work together with less conflict in the future. It may end up that the two of you simply agree to disagree, but even that understanding can help smooth things out for you on your path toward getting your raise.

You may even need to speak with a professional therapist about letting go of past hurts or disappointments. Do not be ashamed of this need or afraid to find someone to help you through these issues. Change is difficult, and getting help is a smart, humble way to approach problems. Your company may even have a counselor on-staff to help with exactly these kinds of issues. If you do not feel comfortable looking for professional help this way, you can find plenty of therapeutic resources on the Internet. Getting professional help can lead you toward a more positive attitude toward your life and work, and possibly a more positive outcome when you ask your boss for your raise.

Take Care of Yourself

We have examined how to take care of your work, how to make your boss happy, and even how to smooth things over with difficult co-workers. However, you will have a much more difficult time taking care of all of these other issues if you do not take care of yourself. You are the most important part of this equation, and you must attend to your own personal needs.

Sleep

The amount of sleep each of us needs is determined in part by age, general health, and lifestyle. You may feel fine with more or less sleep than someone else, but doctors generally recommend that people try to get about eight hours of sleep a night. This is the average amount of sleep that an average person needs to sleep a night to wake up and feel refreshed and alert throughout the day.

Not sleeping enough can have serious consequences, and many of these consequences can directly affect your ability to perform in the office. Reduced sleep can lead to reduced alertness, impaired memory, and a lessened ability to store, use, and process information. However, there can be even more serious consequences, including migraine headaches, a weakened immune system, mood changes, and instability.

It is not always possible to get yourself to bed on time. The occasional important project may keep you at the office longer or get you there earlier than you would like. But you should take care to get the right amount of sleep as often as possible.

Additionally, it is not only the quantity, but the quality of sleep that matters. What you do as you get ready for sleep can greatly affect the quality of the sleep you have, and bad sleep can be just as damaging as not enough sleep. The following tips can help you sleep better and thus perform better at the office.

- **Avoid caffeine and alcohol close to bedtime.** The reason to avoid caffeine may seem obvious. The same jolt that gets you up in the morning can keep you awake at night. Or if you get to sleep, that caffeine may interrupt your natural sleep cycles, making your sleep less effective. Coffee is the clear caffeine culprit, but teas and chocolates may also contain caffeine. Take care to avoid eating these things in the evening, or choose caffeine-free alternatives.

- **Alcohol can also interrupt your sleep cycle.** You may find that a few drinks make you drowsy, but medical experts say that alcohol can actually increase the number of times you wake up during the night. Sometimes, these moments of wakefulness are so slight that the sleeper may not consciously notice that he or she is waking. But the effect on the body will occur whether you realize it or not.

- **Skimp on the spices.** Spicy food can liven up a meal, but it can also keep you up at night. Spicy foods can be difficult for the body to digest and may lead to heartburn. Heartburn tends to get worse when you lie down, so a spicy meal can make it difficult for you to fall asleep.

- **Keep your gauge on half-full.** Eating too much food too close to bedtime can make it difficult to fall asleep. If you are feeling hungry late in the evening, have a small, simple, easy-to-digest snack to tide you over until the morning.

- **Quit smoking.** This is obviously much easier said than done. The journey to smoking cessation can be a long one. But in addition to lung and respiratory health benefits, putting away your packs can help you sleep. Nicotine is a stimulant like caffeine, and as such, it can have similar effects on your sleep patterns, especially if you typically have a cigarette — or several — before bed.

- **Get moving.** Exercise during the day can help you sleep better at night. Just 30 minutes of active exercise can improve your sleep habits — and your health in general. Combine aerobic exercise with some strength-building exercises, and you have a recipe for better health and good sleep. Of course, you should consult with a physician before starting any new exercise program. Make sure you are in a healthy-enough condition to begin exercise.

- **Stick to a schedule.** As much as you can, you should strive for a consistent schedule of when you go to bed and when you wake up. Moving your sleep schedule all over the place can confuse your body and make it more difficult for you to fall and stay asleep.

- **Turn off the TV.** If you have a television in your bedroom, turn it off before trying to fall asleep. Although a favorite TV show can keep you company before you drift off to sleep, the flickering light from the television can disrupt your sleep cycle.

- **Visit your doctor.** If you feel you are not getting enough sleep, or enough quality sleep, you should schedule an appointment with a doctor to find out why you may be missing out on sleep. You may need a lifestyle change, a prescription, or simply a better pillow or mattress. Your doctor will be able to point you in the right direction and get you sleeping deeply.

Eat right

Eat your vegetables. Eat three square meals a day, or five small meals a day. Some diet trends come and go, but the message remains the same: Everyone needs to eat, so you should eat well. Eating well has many obvious health benefits: energy for your day, fuel for your immune system, protection from disease, and a healthy and balanced feeling to get you through your days. When you eat badly, it is not only reflected in your outer appearance — everything from acne breakouts to weight gain — but you can feel it in your body. A healthy body getting the right fuel can give its owner a zest for life, and a lovely body to carry into the fight at work. Regardless of what trendy diet is in the news at any given time, there are some basic rules for eating well:

- **Eat more fruits and vegetables.** It is unlikely that anyone is eating too many healthy fruits and veggies. Fruits and vegetables can be nutritional powerhouses; they provide plenty of vitamins, minerals, fiber, and water. And they are low-calorie enough that your average eater can enjoy plenty of plant-based meals without worrying about taking in too much.

If the idea of eating fruits and vegetables sounds boring to you, it may be because you are not preparing them correctly. It is easy to overcook veggies and turn them from tasty treats into bland, boring side dishes. Spend some time with cookbooks, experimenting with different tastes. Try a new fruit or vegetable once a week until you have exhausted your local grocer's supply. You may be surprised to find just what you can do with what the earth provides.

• **Limit sweets, salts, and fats.** They may taste delicious, but sugars, sodium, and the many types of fats that exist in some of the food we love can be dangerous. With too many of them, one can develop diabetes, a problem with weight control, insomnia, or heart problems.

One problem with sugars, salts, and fats is that you may not realize just what is in what you are eating. Learn to read food labels and to fully understand them. If a product seems to only have a few grams of fat in it, see whether the label indicates whether that is the total fat content — or the fat content in a serving. It may be that there are several servings in what you are eating, and you may be ingesting much more than you mean to.

The closer to its original form a food is, the fewer additives will have been put into the food. Additives can make food less healthy. For example, a fresh cut of chicken will have less sodium than packaged and sliced chicken. Fresh fruit off the grove stand will not have sugar added to it the way canned fruit often does.

Your body does need a certain amount of sugar, salt, and good fats to function properly, so do not cut them out of your diet completely. Depriving your body of these natural parts of food can be just as destructive as overindulging.

- **Drink more water.** Much like sleep, the amount of water each person needs each day will vary based on age, weight, lifestyle, and genetic predeterminants. Even the weather can affect how much water you need. Lately, research has begun to question the traditional idea that each of us needs eight glasses of water a day. But eight glasses is usually not too much for the average person, so medical professionals continue to suggest drinking plenty of water each day.

  Water hydrates your skin and cells; cushions joints; helps minerals, vitamins, and blood travel around your body; and helps eliminate waste. In contrast, dehydration can make you feel lightheaded and weak, and it can lead to physical discomfort, from dry mouth to muscle cramps, and can even cause changes in your body's chemistry.

- **Enjoy lean protein.** Sources of lean protein, including turkey or chicken breast, beans, and shellfish, can keep you feeling full and give you long-lasting energy, without adding too many calories to your day. Other sources of lean protein include fish, low-fat beef, and non-fat or low-fat dairy products like cheese, milk, and yogurt.

Relax and de-stress

Another important part of taking care of yourself is to let stress go. A certain amount of stress is necessary to keep you motivated to action. But with too much stress, you can experience weight gain or loss, sleepless nights, irritability, and a lack of focus on your work. There are steps you can take to keep your stress in check at work. And if you give yourself some time to unwind and de-stress, your work — and your spirit — will thank you for the time and effort that you put into keeping yourself calm, cool, and collected.

- **Slow and gentle wins the race.** Recent research shows that slow-paced activities, like yoga and gardening, can help bring stress levels down. But do not worry: You do not have to move away and join an ashram — an Indian location of meditation and prayer — or plant acres of farmland. A windowsill garden and a few choice yoga poses once a day can do wonders for bringing your stress levels down.

- **Hobbies that require thoughtfulness can teach your mind to focus completely on tasks.** This helps the hobbyist stop worrying about other issues for a time. Worry can be unproductive, so when you can stop your mind from doing it, you free it up to concentrate on more productive enterprises. Some of these slow-moving, calm-inducing hobbies and activities include painting, knitting or cross-stitching, and listening to classical music.

- **Get some bodywork done.** Your body is your biggest instrument, and the tool you will use most often. You cannot do anything without your body going with you. Even when you sleep or rest, you have to get your body into a comfortable position. And if there is anything wrong with your body, it will let you know and interrupt any sleep you may get. It pays to take care of your body and let it know that it is loved. Aside from eating right and exercising, you should take time to pamper your body as well. You work hard; your body goes through it with you, and it should be rewarded for what it does.

- **Massage.** Whether you prefer an intense deep-tissue, a more gentle Swedish, or a stimulating hot-stone massage, the power of touch can help you work out the kinks and relax after a tough day or week at the office.

- **Manicures and pedicures.** These treatments need not be just for women. Manis and pedis often come with a variety of skin treatments, and even short massages leave you feeling as good as your digits look. You do not even have to get a polish on your fingers and toes. This is good news for the men who might want to give it a try, but who do not want painted nails as a reminder of their foray into relaxation.

- **Lather, rinse, and repeat.** Having someone else do work for you feels good, even if it is work that is as simple as washing your hair. A professional shampoo can leave your locks looking luxurious and your scalp feeling wonderfully tingly. What is even better about a professional shampoo is that if you stick with the basic service, it can be inexpensive.

- **Spend time with friends.** People are social creatures, but the long hours we often put in at the office can separate us from society more than is healthy. It is easy to get quite caught up with duties and obligations, but you must remember to make time to spend designated hours with the people you know and love. Spending time with friends gives you the chance to share your struggles with people who want to help you. You can find support for your struggles, and you can relax and laugh with them as well, which always helps. Spending time with others helps remind you that you are not alone in what you are dealing with and that many people share similar struggles. Plus, it feels good to spend time with people whose affections and adoration you do not have to earn.

- **Live your life to avoid stressors.** There are many active choices that you can make each day to alleviate stress. It may be hard to accept at times, but often, we bring stress upon ourselves with the shortcuts that we try to make work each day. But by incorporating some proactive, positive choices into your daily routine, you can help ward off stressful situations.

    - **If you have enough time, get up 15 minutes earlier than you normally do.** This will give you just enough extra time to get things in order for your day. Though sleep is helpful, oversleeping can eat up precious time and add stress to your day.

    - **Before you go to bed, plan out at least the first part of your day.** Make a mental note as to what you are going to wear and have for breakfast. Relieving yourself of needing to make these decisions when you are groggy from just having woken up can ease early morning stress.

- **Tell the truth.** If you do not tell lies, you will avoid the stress of having to remember what you said.

- **Keep your standards high, but leave room for mistakes.** You are not perfect and never will be, and that is all right. You should always strive to do your best, but forgiving yourself when you make a mistake will help keep the stress of perfectionism out of your life.

- **Look for the good.** Every time something goes wrong, there are more than likely plenty of good things going on around that one mishap. Instead of concentrating on what upset you, look for the positive things.

- **Learn to say "No."** You do not have to take on every task or favor that your friends and family ask of you. Saying "no" when you are busy — or simply need time to yourself — can help ease stress by keeping you from becoming overbooked or overburdened.

- **Delegate.** If a project is taking too much time, or if you simply have too much work to do, there is nothing wrong with sharing that burden, whether the task is housework or a work project. Share the workload with your spouse, significant other, roommate, office mate, or co-worker.

- **Recognize what topics stress you out, and avoid them in conversation.** If talking politics gets your blood boiling, take care to change the conversation if politics comes up. The same goes for any subject about which you feel passionate or sensitive. Deflect the conversation politely to move it on to more neutral subjects.

- **Tell people what you want and need.** No one can help you reach your goals if no one knows what they are. Likewise, no one can help you avoid trouble if they do not know what gives you trouble. Voice your thoughts when you can, and set boundaries so people can avoid topics that get you going.

To review

Before you can move on to an advanced position — whether that is a different job or an increase in pay — you need to demonstrate that you can master the basics of being a business professional. These basics can be defined as your look, your words, and your work. Your employer will examine all these traits when you ask for your raise, so be ready to show them off.

- Your look. Your look includes your clothes, hair, makeup, and anything else about your person — including odors. Take care of all of them.

- You should always dress fittingly for the office. Your clothes should not only be professional, but clean and pressed. Makeup, jewelry, and hairstyles should be conservative and office-appropriate.

- Cologne and perfume should be worn in small amounts.

- Carry deodorants and mints to take care of potentially offensive body and breath odors.

- Your words — both spoken and written — should stand out. And not because they are full of mistakes.

  - During meetings, make sure that your voice is heard. Speak politely and professionally to everyone involved. Acknowledge contributions made by other co-workers and executives to give your own words even more power.

  - On the phone, make sure you communicate clearly, as your listener does not have the benefit of making eye contact with you. Ask clear questions, and repeat and rephrase answers to make sure you have clearly understood the information presented to you.

    - Your outgoing message should clearly identify you to anyone who is calling.

- When leaving a message, make sure to leave your name, contact information, and a summary of why you are calling.

- When writing letters, drafting memos, typing e-mails, and sending faxes, make sure your correspondence is properly formatted, easy to read, and error-free.

  - Print your communication and read it on hard copy. This will help you catch typos.

  - Do not rely on spell-check programs to find all your mistakes. It is also possible that your spell-check program may change things that were correct to begin with. Spell checkers are helpful for catching many mistakes, but should not be used in place of human evaluation.

  - Though e-mails can be sent quickly, do not allow yours to become sloppy or unprofessional. An e-mail should get the same care that a business letter gets before being sent.

- Sounding like a professional means using correct grammar and business-related terminology.

- Take care to learn the vernacular related to your business. You can brush up on this language by reading trade publications and documents created by your company.

- Make sure your grammar is correct when dealing with other business people. It is possible that you speak more casually when you are not at work. While that is fine to do with friends, it will weaken you in your employer's eyes. Brush up on your language skills, and use them at the office.

- In addition to looking good and speaking well, you should make sure you are doing your work well.

  - Keeping your workspace organized will allow you to work more efficiently and with fewer errors.

  - Leave personal items away from your main work area. Keep them where they will not distract you and where you can be sure they are safe.

  - Avoid hoarding paperwork. Important papers should be filed, and papers that are not necessary should be discarded.

  - Keep phone and e-mail messages organized and filed in a way that makes them easy to reference, until the matters to which they refer are completed.

  - Prioritize your work so that important or sensitive matters are attended to and do not get lost in the shuffle.

  - Use stress to your advantage. Clearly, you should not make yourself sick with worry, but understanding that things need to get done can encourage you to work more efficiently.

- Learning to use keyboard shortcuts instead of always reaching for your mouse can shave precious seconds off of your work load. A few seconds here and there may not seem like much, but over time, those seconds will add up to increased efficiency.

- Stop distractions before they stop you. Turning off e-mail alerts, putting your personal cell phone on silent, and arriving early to work can help you get work done without being bothered by typical distractions. The less distracted you are, the more efficiently you will be able to work.

- Keep a positive attitude. It will make getting work done easier, and others will appreciate your upbeat spirit.

- Learn to see challenges as opportunities. Rather than seeing challenges as obstacles to slow you down, see them as a chance to prove your problem-solving skills.

- Enjoy working hard. Every job, no matter how tedious, has its merit. If you learn to see the benefits of every task you do, you will have an easier time getting through them.

- Be humble. Understand that you will always have things to learn, and you will not always have all the answers. Do not be afraid to ask for help or clarification. Keeping a sincere, humble attitude will lead others to appreciate you more.

- Let go of past issues so that you can move on. Stop beating yourself up for mistakes you made in the past. Also, stop beating up others for things they may have done to you. Work to resolve conflicts with fellow employees so that you can concentrate on what is ahead of you instead of wallowing in what is behind.

- Take care of yourself. You will not be able to focus on your work if you are not attending to your own personal needs.

  - Sleep well. Try to get around eight hours of sleep a night. Avoid eating too much before bedtime, and turn off the television so you can sleep deeply without waking up during the night.

  - Eat for your health. Eating a balanced diet will help your body run smoothly. And when your body is in balance, you will have a better time working to the best of your abilities.

  - Relax and de-stress. Though a certain amount of stress can help keep you motivated, too much of it can be harmful to your health. Take steps to give your body, mind, and spirit time to relax and unwind so that you can more effectively return to concentrating on work when it is time to work.

CASE STUDY: SHELBY SMITH

Shelby Smith
General manager
Clinton, Tennessee

Shelby Smith, general manager of Newport Precision, Inc., which manufactures automotive machinery, explains that the most common mistake an employee makes when asking for a raise varies based on whether the employee is salaried or hourly. Often, people who are paid hourly comment, "I will work harder if you pay me more," or salaried employees just ask for a pay raise without providing data to back up the value in return for the pay raise.

Regarding body language during a meeting with an employee, Smith confirms that it does play a role. "Being too aggressive or arrogant, or being too shy or withdrawn, gives the wrong impression. Either they are trying to force you into it (giving a pay raise), or they really don't think they deserve it. A confident disposition should be the employee's goal," Smith said.

Smith expects an employee asking for a pay raise to have some justification as to why they think they deserve the raise. "Even if I do not agree, it shows their thought process and how they think about themselves in relation to the job," Smith said.

CHAPTER 9

Brand Yourself

Picture stocked grocery store aisles. It is likely that the products that immediately come to mind are the ones with a strong brand identity — the ones with the most unique packaging, an easily remembered slogan, or a celebrity endorsement. We immediately recognize, remember, and consider certain items because the companies behind them have spent time and money to make their products stand out. Likewise, it is not enough to simply be a good worker; you have to take the time and energy to let others know what a strong asset you are.

Manage Expectations

If your company has expectations of you that you are not meeting, it will not matter how well you do the work that you are doing. If it is not what your boss wants from you, you will fall below his or her expectations. Likewise, if you are doing much more than is expected of you, but you are not letting your supervisor know what you are up to, your supervisor may think well of you, but not as highly as he or she ought to.

To effectively manage the expectations your supervisor — and thus your company — has of you, you need to schedule some time to sit down with your manager to discuss these expectations. Let your manager know that you are interested in discussing your duties and goals, just to make sure you are giving what he or she wants from you.

When you know what your managers want from you, you can immediately decide what you need to do to meet and exceed their expectations. Knowing what your supervisor actually expects will prevent you from doing too much. Letting your boss know you are working toward meeting his or her expectations will make him or her aware of you and what you are doing. It will also encourage your boss to help you meet your collective goals.

Discussing your company's expectations and your ability to meet them can also prevent you from falling short of their desires. Say there are four main goals your employer has for you this term, but you only feel comfortable with three of them. You will be a stronger employee if you are honest about what you feel you can handle. If you take on more than you are able, all of the work will suffer. If you sit down and discuss what is expected of you, you have the chance to let your employer know what challenges you and the opportunity to find solutions. Trying to work beyond your means may hinder your performance and, thus, your chance at earning a raise.

Thin the Herd

Because employers like to feel that their staff members are special or unique, you should do what it takes to make yourself stand out from the rest of your peers. When you rise above what the average worker in your position is doing, your employer will notice you. Making yourself one of a few employees who stand out from the rest will put you in a stronger position to receive your raise.

The best way to make yourself stand out is to do the work better. Use the tips in the previous section to make sure your work is delivered in a timely manner and is error-free. Organize your work life so you have the extra few minutes to inspect each aspect of your work and correct anything that needs attention. Your employer will appreciate the effort and will be keen to reward you for it.

Another way to make yourself stand out from your peers is to identify problems and offer solutions. Make sure the problem you identify is something within the scope of your duties. Take the time to notice whether files are as organized as they could be; whether scheduling procedures are as streamlined as they could be; or whether a staggered lunch break system would allow your office to better handle attending to customer concerns.

Many people allow problems to hold them back, but companies need people who can work to overcome problems as soon as they are perceived. Problem-solvers are strong assets to any company. Make yourself a problem-solver, and you will be well on your way to a raise. And the more frequently you find solutions to problems, the easier solving problems in the future will become.

Once you identify a problem, make a list of several solutions for it. Bring these suggestions to your supervisor in a sincere, non-aggressive way. Your employer will appreciate your attention to detail, and if your solutions work, you make him or her look better in the process.

Companies want to know their employees are capable of doing more than the tasks they are specifically given. They want to know that the people working for them have a sense of upward mobility. Identifying and offering solutions to problems is an excellent way to prove you meet these criteria.

Make sure not to name-call or point fingers in the process. You should avoid saying things like, "Matthew is not working hard enough. I think if we give him a shorter lunch, he will be more productive." Do not make the problems that you find personal or about any one employee; this will make you look petty and gossipy. The problems that you identify should be about procedure, organization, or communication — business concerns that anyone would agree with.

Using the suggestions already discussed in this book will put you in an enormous position to stand out as an employee. Choose to be the one of your peers with developed communication skills, superior organizational ability, and a keen eye that can trouble-shoot for the executives. Doing so will make you stand out from the rest of the pack and will put you in an excellent position to ask for and receive a raise.

Get Them Talking

It is not enough that you know what a quality employee you are. Your supervisors and their supervisors need to know what a quality employee you are as well. To spread the word, you need to market yourself and get them talking.

You may think that your bosses are well-aware of what you are doing and all the wonderful things you have done before, but all employees are busy, and your supervisor may not have information about you right at the top of his or her head. It is your responsibility to make sure your boss has this information on hand.

An excellent, easy way to let your boss know about the successes you are having in the office is to schedule some time to review your goals and objectives. This allows you to lead into the discussion with a statement like this: "Since Mr. Thompson was so happy with the work I did on his account, I wanted to make sure I was rising to the same standard on this project." A statement like this will remind your boss of the good work you did recently. It will also allow them to direct you as to how you can continue doing good work in the future.

Once you open the dialogue about the work you have done, ask your supervisor leading questions so he or she will talk about it more. Some questions to ask are:

- What can I do in the next step to ensure my success?

- What do you think is the strongest part of this presentation?
- How can I earn more projects like this?

You may also ask your immediate supervisor to recommend you to a higher executive or another supervisor for similar work or to allow you to shadow a higher-level project. A recommendation will get your supervisor talking about you to the person whom he or she reports to. And as long as your boss has good things to say, you are one step closer to earning your raise.

The name of the game is networking. People are not going to find you; you have to go to people and let them know who you are. Networking can be stressful for many people, but it is a necessary part of being successful in business. Networking can, for many, bring up images of smarmy business people making boozy small talk over drinks. But effective networking is a powerful tool. It can help remind those in charge of who and where you are — and allow them to help you get to where you want to be.

Networking frequently asked questions

Do I need business cards?

Yes. Depending on your position at the company, you may have business cards supplied to you by your employer. If you are not one of these employees, you will need to order your own business cards. It is worth checking with your company to see whether cards can be ordered on your behalf. If not, there are many printers who will print a large number of cards for a reasonable amount of money.

You can personalize the cards to your liking. You may choose to have your cards identify closely with your company, or you may choose to add your own personal flair. Either way, you should have business cards on you at all times.

Your cards should include contact information — a phone number and e-mail address for sure. You may include a mailing address if you are comfortable doing so. You want your cards to make it easy for people to remember who you are, what you do, and how they can get in touch with you if they need to. It does not matter as much how fancy the paper is, though you should take care to use a solid card stock. Cards printed off your home printer on flimsier paper will look unprofessional and cheap. The cards do not need to be fancy linen with watermarks, but they should be on sturdy paper and easy to read.

Having a business card ready implies that you are someone whom people want to stay in touch with, so make sure you always carry some with you; you never know when you will have the chance to discuss business with someone. Getting caught without a business card at a professional or networking event will allow you to be easily forgotten.

Do I need a Web page?

A Web page is not necessary, but can be a good tool for marketing yourself. Do not worry about creating a complicated Web page with layers of interactive links, images, and graphics. A simple Web presence can solidify your professional image and give potential employers, mentors, and clients a way to get in touch with you. All you need is contact information and a brief listing of your accomplishments to get you started.

There are many books that can guide you through the creation of your own Web page. If you are not a skilled programmer or Web designer, many of these books will be enough to get you set up with a simple page that gets your basic point across. However, if you are looking to create something more interactive, it may be in your best interest to hire a designer or a firm to do the work for you. Hiring a professional will cost you some money, but it may save time and can ensure that your page looks professional.

Besides developing a Web page, you may also want to take time to clean up your potential Web presence. Because so much information, from news reports to vacation photos, is digitized and put into cyberspace, there may be considerable information about you floating around. Type your name into several search engines and see what comes up. If there are things you can control — such as an embarrassing photo on your friend's blog page — do what you need to do to remove this information. If your friends or family have pictures of you online that paint you in a less-than-professional light, ask them to remove the images. If you have a blog in your name that rants and raves about any topic, experiment with a pseudonym, or disable the page. The Internet may seem like a place to deposit images of the fun times you have had, but you do not want stray images or information to make you look unprofessional.

One more note on your Web presence — make sure your e-mail address is something that a professional would respect. Your e-mail address should also be something that is easy to remember. A simple variation of your name is the best way to go for business purposes.

Can I drink alcohol at company events?

Many company-sponsored events, especially those in the evening, may feature an open bar or otherwise reduced cost for alcohol. While it may be tempting to take advantage of such a situation, alcohol will not be your friend at a company event. You will want to have all your wits about you as you navigate the party or dinner. Off-hour events are fantastic places to meet and mingle, and you will want to be remembered for your interesting conversation and dazzling smile, not as the employee who seemed a little "off" that night.

What do I talk about when networking?

You should always have some neutral topics of discussion that you feel comfortable speaking on at the ready. Avoid launching into passionate diatribes and soapbox speeches about politics, religion, or social issues — anything that could potentially be divisive in mixed company. You should be aware of news, current events, and some pop culture references as well.

It pays do to a little digging before going to an event. Find out some key players who will be in attendance, and take some time to learn more about them. That way, you can ask specific questions that should appeal to their egos. People love to talk about themselves, so ask plenty of open-ended questions about their work, and you will have a good way to keep the conversation going.

How can I avoid coming across as needy or looking for a handout?

One way to make sure you are giving while you are trying to get is to make sure that you talk up your strong points. It is possible that you have a skill or expertise that may be in demand. Do not only ask questions of your superiors: Talk up your own skills, and let it be known that people may need you as much as you know you need other people.

I am naturally quiet. Will my work speak for itself so I do not have to?

No, it will not. The business world is a fast-paced place, and what happens one day may be immediately forgotten the next. You will definitely want to remind whom you can when you can about your accomplishments, goals, and abilities.

Also, although you may be quiet, there are plenty of people who are not. Those people will outshine your demeanor if your demeanor is quieter. Those forward personalities will not stop to help you find your footing at a meeting, so rise to the occasion, step forward, and let them know you can shine just as brightly.

Strengthen Your Relationship

You do not need to hang out with your boss every weekend, but it is in your best interest to make a personal connection with your managers and supervisors. Allowing your managers to know a little bit about you — and you getting to know a little bit about your managers and supervisors — will make it more likely for you to get your raise. It is easier for your boss to reward someone he or she knows well, trusts, and can see spending a large amount of time with in the future.

As you get to know your boss, it is important to make your efforts sincere. If you are simply sucking up to make yourself look good, your efforts will feel insincere and will do you more harm than good. On the other hand, if you approach your supervisor with a genuine spirit of camaraderie, you will find yourself closer to your boss and one step closer to your raise.

Approaching your supervisor on a personal level should be done at the right time. You should not ask personal questions during meetings or while your boss is conducting important business. Asking your boss to lunch is completely acceptable, and during that lunch is an excellent time to talk more personally.

A good way to ask your supervisors to lunch is to tell them you want to get some advice on a project or on your career track. Going to lunch with your boss under the guise of a business discussion will always give you something to fall back on if the conversation stalls. Also, it will let your boss know that you are interested in moving forward in your career.

When you go to lunch, do not simply launch into intensely per-sonal questions about your boss's life. Instead, ask open-ended questions that will allow your boss to talk about himself or her-self. Also, ask questions that will result in a positive answer. For example, do not say, "What do you most dislike about your job?" Instead, try, "What are some challenges you have enjoyed overcoming in this field?" If your questions call for a positive response, your lunch will be more pleasant, and your boss will associate talking about positive things with you; in turn, he or she will think of your more positively.

According to Anna Post, author and spokesperson for The Emily Post Institute, it can be awkward if you do not have a reason for asking your boss to lunch, and it can leave you looking direction-less. You need to have a reason for asking for some of their time.

"Lunch is usually a time to take it to the next level," said Post. "That may be in part my personal opinion, but I have a feeling that the dynamic of a younger employee asking an older employee out to lunch suggests that this needs to be more private or personal than a meeting in an office, which suggests to me that it needs to be a bigger level of discussion."

Being the host

The person inviting is the person hosting, and the host is the one who pays. If you asked for the lunch meeting, the burden to pay is on you. But do not fight your boss if he or she offers to pay. You can counter once, then leave it alone, and thank them if they insist.

To choose a place to eat, you need to suggest something you can afford. If you want to give them a choice, give maybe two restaurants. People often have an easier time choosing from two concrete choices.

If you are both leaving the office, it certainly makes sense to go together, whether that involves walking, taking a cab, or driving. As the host, you should offer to drive.

The conversation

With dinner, you wait until after dinner to get down to business. You are there to share the meal; you have more time to talk about it. But people's days are busy, and with breakfast, brunch, or lunch, you need to get down to business once you have ordered.

Once the waiter has taken away the menus, it is time to get down to business.

Having a few topics up your sleeve — such as pop culture, sports, or another topic of common interest — is a good way to make small talk. Another technique is to ask people questions or their opinions about various topics. It is a sign of your business skills that you can keep the conversation running well.

Diaries are Not Just for Teenagers

A helpful way to track your work, progress, and any problems you overcome is to document your work days. At the beginning of the work day, make a list of your tasks, duties, and anything else you hope to accomplish. As the day goes on, check off what you complete, and make any notes that would be helpful to reference later. These notes may include the time it took you to finish, any praise or comments you received from your employer, or any difficulties you found with the task. Documenting what you do each day will help you to remember the good work you have done and have it at ready when you go to ask for your raise.

You should also include others in your personal paper trail. If you have a conversation with your boss about an assignment or project he or she wants you to take on, send an e-mail when you are back at your workspace. In the e-mail, reiterate the terms of the project and any notes, direction, or instruction your boss gave to you. This will ensure that both of you are on the same page so there will be no surprises about expectations. This will also give you an opportunity to show how you exceeded expectations, should that be the case when the project is finished. An example of such an e-mail would read like this:

Mr. Cortez,

I am looking forward to working on the Adamski project. Below is my understanding of the details per our recent conversation. Please let me know if I have missed anything.

- Secure vendors for Friday launch party
- Prepare gift bags for sponsors
- Proofread invitations and mail by Tuesday

The details of each job, project, and task will differ, and it is crucial to make sure you and your employer both agree on what those details are. If not, you may fall short of expectations without realizing it, hurting your chances of getting a raise. This kind of paper trail also protects you from anyone saying you did not complete a task as assigned.

It is also helpful to include "extracurricular" goals on your list. Challenge yourself to speak to someone new in the office. Try to make time to read the company newsletter. If you normally eat lunch off-site, make an effort to eat in a common area and get to know someone new. Giving yourself these daily goals will make you a stronger employee.

At the end of the day, review your list of duties, tasks, and goals. See what you were able to accomplish, and make any helpful notes about it. Keep this running list of what you have done each day in a file that you can easily access. You will need it when you make your presentation for your raise.

If you were unable to attend to something, make a note as to why. Did you give yourself too many things to get to in a day? Did one task take longer than you expected? Were you sidetracked with unexpected work? Understanding why you were not able to complete a task will help you better plan for it in the future. It may also help you discover a problem with procedure that you can discuss with your boss.

To Review

Food and clothing items with strong brand identities stand out at the store, and you can use the same principles to make you and your work stand out at the office. Branding yourself is not just something extra to do; it is good business sense, and something every up-and-coming employee should spend time doing.

- Meet with your supervisor to discuss what his or her expectations are of you. You may not even realize you are not rising to meet their expectations, or your supervisor may not be aware of the fact that you are regularly exceeding expectations. Either way, a face-to-face conversation with your supervisor can get you both on the same page regarding your work and job performance.

- Find ways to take on responsibilities that your peers are not taking on. Take the time to develop additional skills that your peers may not have. Doing more than your peers is a good way to make yourself stand out from the herd.

- Open up a dialogue with your supervisor about your work and goals. Find ways to get your boss talking about you and what you have done. If you can encourage your supervisor to discuss you in a positive light, that is a strong business move.

- A strong relationship with your supervisor will not guarantee a raise for you, but it will put you in a more likely position to receive one. Taking your boss out for lunch, setting meetings with him or her on company time, and attending company-sponsored events are strong ways to ensure you and your boss have time to get to know each other.

- Keep a journal of the work you do each day. Take care to note any accomplishments and who was involved. You will need to refer to this document when you petition for your raise. Having this information at the ready will make it easier for you to take your case to your boss, and it will give you the encouragement you need to keep going strong and working hard.

CHAPTER 10

Tailor Yourself to Meet Their Needs

Just like in a romantic relationship, both parties have to meet each other's needs for your business relationship to work. While important, it is not enough to be a good employee; you also have to be the kind of employee that your company is looking for. Each company and business has a different culture inside its offices with different priorities and goals. You will need to find out what your company is specifically looking for to make itself grow, and adjust yourself to fit into those wants and needs.

As with branding yourself, it is not enough to do the work and not be prepared to show it off. This chapter will show you how to identify what your company is looking for in its employees and how to build a cache of materials that prove you have it. This is a crucial part of the case you will build to earn your raise.

Research

Take the time to learn about the people in your company. Find out who the big players and major decision-makers are — and how they got there. A good way to learn this information is through face-to-face communication. Asking for a lunch or informal informational meeting with these high-ranking employees is not only a good way to get the information you are looking for; it will also give you a personal connection to those who will be making decisions about your raise. However, it is not always possible to get these kinds of meetings in a timely manner. If that is the case, you should look for information about these people in company research materials or online.

Find out about what the company values outside of the office by learning where it sends its money — namely, charities, sponsorships, and investments. While companies will likely give money to a wide range of events and organizations, there tends to be some rhyme or reason to it. Your company will give money to organizations that it thinks will reflect positively on it. By examining where your company's money goes, you can find out what issues and groups are important to your company. And by expressing your own interest in these things, you will make it clear that you are someone your company will want to work with for a while to come.

Research the other guys. Find out what your company's competition is doing and how your company feels about it. By reading trade publications, you can find out where your company ranks in terms of other similar companies. Knowing where your company stands will help you strengthen your case for your raise. If your company is having a rough time, and you have ideas that will help, you have a good case for your raise. If your company is doing well, they will probably be looking to expand and keep the momentum going by promoting new talent.

Get Good at What They Want

You should have a good handle on all the basic office skills — organization, written and oral communication, and time management — but your company may value one of these over the other, or value something else over the basics. You need to find out what those values are and develop your skills in those areas.

If you work for a creative company, it is possible that they want to know that their employees will regularly generate new, innovative ways of doing things. You may be a whiz at formatting, but in this situation, that is not the company's priority; the same is true if you work for a business that has rigid rules about procedure and style. For example, at a law firm, your creative juices may not be as appreciated as your eye for detail. Learn to develop the skills that your company is looking for.

In this process, however, do no shirk your other skills. For example, even if your work is highly creative, format and style are still important. When you ask for your raise, it will be helpful to show that not only can you rise to their creative standards, but you also have an eye for detail that assures that the creative work is presented flawlessly. Likewise, if your place of employment is strict with formatting, style, and presentation rules, it will be a strong move to show that while you allot plenty of time to follow the rules, you are still able to brainstorm creative solutions to problems.

Training and Education

Extra training and education will make you a stronger employee. All industries and technologies are constantly changing, and staying on top of those changes ensures that your skills will mature as the technology does. Most knowledge and learning has a shelf life of just a few years. This means that what you learn today may become irrelevant quickly. Getting a handle on changes in business and technology will keep you on par with newer — and younger — employees, and put you ahead of your peers.

The first and most obvious choice is to go back to school. Enroll in applicable classes at a local college or university. Many schools offer night and weekend classes for working profession-als. Schools also offer certificate programs — courses of study that take much less time than earning a degree, but still give the student plenty of new knowledge and skills. Taking advan-tage of these programs will give you an edge when asking for your raise.

Going back to school does cost money, but many companies will subsidize their employees' continued education. It is in a company's best interest to make sure that its employees are at the top of their game. Helping their employees with financing their education is a strong move on their part.

Many companies offer internal training programs for their employees. These programs can either focus on skills directly necessary to do the work the company does, or they can be tangentially related, such as a language course. Either way, attending these classes can be a good way to freshen up your skills and get to know others in the company at the same time.

Before you go back to school, make sure you know what kind of schooling will work best for your situation. While a graduate degree is a nice accolade, pursuing such a goal will require considerable dedication and time. You may be able to increase your cache with some classes. Many schools even offer certifications that show you have completed a certain amount of training in a particular field. These certifications give you an educational edge without the expense and commitment of an entire degree program. However, some companies are quite excited to welcome new MBAs or Ph.D.s to their staff. Speak with your company and a college admissions counselor about your career goals to help you determine what the best course of action will be for you.

CASE STUDY: KATHY WALDEN

Kathy Walden
Tyler, Texas

Kathy Walden, of Tyler, Texas, tells of her journey to "Bachelorhood," when she returned to school for her bachelor's degree.

"In the fall of 1997, after I was already a wife and mother, my journey to Bachelorhood began again. It had originally started after high school. I graduated from high school in a small town in North Carolina. I packed off to college with high hopes from my family and a future bright and shiny with promise. However, during my second week in attendance at college, I met the man who, 11 months later, would become my husband. My journey to Bachelorhood was detoured by marriage and a job in retail to support my new husband as he completed his degree.

"During that time, Bachelorhood was never far from my mind. My lineage included a long line of credentialed ancestors. My mother, after recovering from a life-threatening house fire, went back to graduate school and earned a degree in library science. I also had an uncle who was a Tuskegee Airman, shot down over Turkey in WWII. I wanted to feel like I belonged to such a brave and courageous family, and somehow, I felt a degree was essential."

After Walden's husband graduated from college, they moved out of the state. School was always on her mind, but life seemed to keep getting in the way. They were saving for a house, so while her husband accepted his first professional job, she settled into a job at a local hospital. Shortly thereafter, they learned they were expecting a daughter.

When their daughter was about two years old, Walden enrolled at a local university. However, she contracted a severe illness and was forced to leave school in order to recover.

Her husband's career caused them to move again. After many years in their third city together, she enrolled at another local university and finally achieved her goal. She graduated with a bachelor's degree in business administration with an emphasis in accounting.

Walden said she does not regret it taking her a little longer than others to complete her journey to get a bachelor's degree. Instead, it helped her discover she was a much more committed, serious student in her 40s than she was when she was 18.

CASE STUDY: KATHY WALDEN

"My self-worth increased immeasurably after earning my degree," Walden said. "I had set a goal and achieved it. My position, at least in my own mind, with my ancestry was at last on par. My sense of accomplishment was enormous. Even now, during down moments, I retreat to the memory of my graduation, and my spirits and determination are reinforced."

"I believe I am now a better employee for having gone back to school, period," Walden explained. "The experience of higher education teaches more than just a vocation or facts. It teaches acceptance and appreciation of people who are different from ourselves. It teaches broad-based thinking about the world and our place in it. It teaches determination to work through obstacles and challenges. These skills and more make us more valuable as employees. Outside-the-box, flexible, and broad-minded individuals grow businesses and corporations. The journey to 'Bachelorhood' builds people, communities, corporations, and nations."

Walden said she learned three important lessons while on the journey. "First, the journey is everything. All of the experiences along the way are valuable. They have shaped my character and deepened my belief in my own abilities. Second, I learned that doubt and fear are the two biggest thieves of joy from our lives. Put these deceptions under your feet and use them for stepping stones for the next achievement," she advised.

"Finally, I learned that age doesn't matter. What does matter is attitude. Set your sights on the stars and soar."

According to Walden, going back to school at an "advanced" age was not easy, but it was worth the trip. She said at her current, even more "advanced" age, she cannot wait to see what happens on her journey to "MastersLand."

"Updating your training and education is not just about going back to school," Walden said. "While taking classes at a local college or university is a strong option, there are others as well. Real-life experience is just as valuable, if not more, than sitting in a classroom. Spending time with other professionals, sitting in on presentations, and interviewing senior employees at your company is a terrific way to learn more about your business. Seeing the skills put to use in real-life situations will give you a leg up that you cannot get simply sitting inside a classroom."

Education is not limited to gaining the specific pieces of information that you will need to do your job. Having a wide frame of reference for current events, news, other cultures, and trends in many fields is all part of being a model employee. Businesses want employees who are caught up on current events, who can discuss issues apart from the specific tasks at hand, and who can see how all the pieces of society are interconnected — and that means staying on top of many things.

There are many ways to increase your frame of reference outside of your specific job. Read the newspaper and listen to news radio in your car. Listen to radio talk shows on both sides of the issues — this will give you perspective and make you better able to empathize with opinions that you may not necessarily agree with. Listen to audio books as you drive. Everything from classics in literature to current best sellers to language programs can increase your frame of reference. Attend community and cultural events. This kind of commitment to learning will make you an employee that your supervisors cannot ignore.

CASE STUDY: STEPHEN C. ELDRIDGE

Stephen C. Eldridge
Tax attorney & public accountant
Cosby, Tennessee

According to Stephen C. Eldridge, a retired tax attorney and certified public accountant from New York, performance-yielding profits are what earn an employee a pay raise. He says when an employee asks for a pay raise, he or she should provide "a brief recitation of the justification, with paperwork on the details available."

Mistakes an employee should avoid when asking for a pay raise include not being totally prepared to make his or her "case," not being dressed professionally or appropriately, and being overly aggressive, said Eldridge.

Organizational skills are critical when an employee wants to climb the career ladder, he said, and the right time to ask for a pay raise is during the annual performance review — an employee should not ask for a pay raise until he or she has worked for the company a year.

Eldridge said the most common mistake employees make when asking for a pay raise is having a lack of self-confidence when presenting the facts to support his or her case.

"Body language has a significant impact on a meeting where an employee is pursuing a raise. Persistent body language is required to convey proper confidence."

He added that budgetary limits most often prevent supervisors from giving employees pay raises.

CHAPTER 11

Prepare and Assemble Your Case

You have done the background work, decided what your goals and needs are, and made sure your work is up to par. Now you need to put your information together in a way that will appeal to your boss. The presentation is just as important as the preparation. The following section will guide you through this procedure.

Review Your Review

Asking for a review will likely cause your employer to immediately examine your last performance review. Beat them to the punch and review it yourself. This will give you the chance to prop up the positive items on your review and prepare answers for any marks against you.

It is easy to obtain a copy of your review. You should have been given a copy the last time your boss sat down with you to discuss it. If you did not receive a copy, or if you have misplaced yours, simply ask your human resources department for another; then be sure to make an extra copy of it. You should keep one for yourself to make notes on and have a clean copy to give to your boss with your presentation materials. On the copy you give to your boss, you may want to highlight areas that make you stand out, such as high marks, positive comments, and any awards or official recognition you have received for your work.

Make note of the positive comments in your review, and be careful not to slack off in these areas. It can be easy to become too comfortable with things that come naturally to us. Just because your boss said you were doing something well on your review does not mean he or she cannot change his or her mind if you become lackadaisical in pursuing these items.

You should also be prepared to discuss anything negative on your review. Before you speak to your employer about your raise, make sure you have answers for poorer performance in whatever areas were indicated on your review. Always be ready to answer these issues with positive statements that show growth and improvement. For example, if time management was a problem, you should be ready to say something like, "Now that I understand how much time each of these tasks take, I am able to successfully plan my day accordingly." Never make excuses for less-than-shining performances. Do not give your bosses answers like, "Well, I was going through a hard time then." Your boss may be kind, but when it comes to giving you a raise, he or she will want to know that you can succeed at your job in spite of personal issues.

Side-by-Side Comparison

One of the strongest pieces of evidence that you deserve a raise — assuming your work quality is high — is that people doing the same job at other places are getting paid more. This will cause your perceived value to rise in your boss's mind. It will also show that an employee with your skills and qualifications is a valuable commodity that deserves to be well-compensated.

Though you should have salary information ready to present to your boss, you should never present it as a threat. You should also avoid directly comparing yourself to other people in your office. You should present this information as a set of objective facts to demonstrate trends in your field.

You can opt to show this information however you like. If your boss is a visual person, you may opt for a graph. A bar graph or a line graph showing where your salary is relative to salaries at other firms could be an effective way of making your point. A graph is clear and immediately easy to understand. But if your boss is more of a numbers person, simply listing your salary and where it falls relative to other salaries can do the job just as well. However you choose to illustrate your point, it should be clear that one of your points is that your salary is not up to par with current industry standards.

It may be, of course, that your salary is in the high range of salaries for your field. If this is the case, it will be best to leave this information out of your presentation. A salary comparison will be most effective when your salary is not in line with industry norms and means. If it turns out that you are not able to use salary information as part of the case for your raise, do not worry. There will be plenty of other pieces of supporting material to bolster your case.

Recommendation Letters

Another important part of your presentation package will be letters of recommendation. These letters can be written by supervisors or clients. Your boss will expect you to speak highly of yourself, but others joining in through positive letters they have written on your behalf will strengthen your case.

To make the letters have the strongest impact, you will need to make sure you get them in a timely manner. You will also need to make sure they include all the information that will be most helpful to you. This will require clear communication on your part when you ask references for these letters.

The first people you should ask for recommendation letters are supervisors or higher-ranking employees at your company that you have worked with. These people will know about the corporate culture at your business and will also understand what will be important to those making decisions about your raise. Thus, they will be able to easily tailor their letters to your purpose.

Next, you should go to clients or customers — people you have done work with through your company. These contacts are important because a company will want to know you can work with people outside your organization to get the job done. These letters will speak to your service ability and will explain how you are seen outside the company's walls.

Finally, you may want to consider getting general letters of reference from people who may know you better than your employers or clients. Personal recommendation letters or letters that speak to your character will provide your employer with a different perception of you than they may get by simply working with you. While these references may not have any idea how your business works or how well you work at it, they will be able to speak to your general character — which is also important to your company.

When you ask for a letter of recommendation, make sure you are clear about what you want. You will need to give your references a time in which to get their letters to you. Make sure you get your letters back in enough time to check for typos and assemble them with your other presentation materials. Let your references know that the letters should be relatively short — no longer than a page. They should also speak to what your reference knows best about you. Your personal reference should not attempt to speak about the inner workings of your business, and your business references should not speak about your personal accomplishments if they are not familiar with them.

After you have received your recommendation letters, proofread them the way you would your own work. Do not assume they are mistake-free. Read them carefully, and if you do find a mistake, politely ask your reference to correct it. Chances are, the letter is in a computer file somewhere, and it will not take long to correct. You may also offer to re-type the letter if time is a concern for your reference.

Always thank your references for their help. This will ensure they will be willing to help you again in the future. Send your references a thank-you note when they are done with their letter. Thank them for their time, and be sure to update them on your status.

Polish Your Trophies and Dust Your Case

Always be ready to speak to your accomplishments. While you may think that others will remember what you have done, the truth is, they probably will not. This is nothing personal against you. People are busy, and bosses change often. The person deciding on your raise may not be the person who hired you. Or if they are, they may have also hired dozens or hundreds of other employees, too. The point is that your good work may get lost in the shuffle. You will need to have a working list of what you have done ready to present to your boss when you ask for your raise.

Your list should include accomplishments big and small. Whether you closed a massive deal or simply streamlined a filing process, you should make note of what you do and how it affects the company. As you check off the items on your to-do list, highlight any that are significant. Record the date, time, and how much time it took to do them. Each month, file the highlighted items in their own file so you can have them ready when you need them.

It is Not You, It is Them

Before you discuss your raise with your employer, make sure you are also ready to discuss the state of your company. How your company is doing financially will have a huge effect on how you approach your boss about your raise. What your company's goals are will affect how you pitch yourself. Remember, your company is ultimately looking out for itself; you will have to show you are also looking out for the company.

Find and understand your company's mission statement. You can get the mission statement from company literature or from the HR department. Read it and make sure you understand what it means. The mission statement will clue you in to what your company values, how it sees itself, and what it hopes to accomplish. Make sure when you discuss your raise with your boss that you demonstrate how you fit into the company's overall goals.

Respect the financial situation your company is in. If it is a lucrative year, do not think you can simply take advantage of the windfall. The company probably already has plenty of things it plans to do with its money. You will need to respectfully explain why they should share their profits with you. Conversely, if it is a financially slow year, make sure you address that as well. Demonstrating that you understand that money may be tight for the company will make you look more like a business person, rather than just an employee with his or her hand out.

If you do not know how the company is doing financially, make it a priority to find out. An informational meeting with your boss or supervisor is a good way to discover this information. Ask how the company is doing this year and whether there were any changes that significantly affected revenue. If you work for a public company, research stock prices and check the shareholders' reports. Whatever method you use, make sure you know how the company is doing, so you will know how to show your boss you can help it do even better.

Finally, do not make your raise about what you need. Ultimately, your company will decide whether to give you a raise or not based on how much it will benefit them. In your reasons for deserving a raise, you need to focus on them, not yourself. Never approach your employer with reasons that involve your personal issues. Do not say you need a raise because you are trying to get out of debt. While this may be true, your personal problems are not your boss's concern. Instead, focus your reasons on how you are benefiting the company.

Name Your Price

As you bring your work up to — and beyond — par and prepare to get your raise, you will need to determine exactly how much you want. It is not enough to tell your boss that you want "more" money; you will need to know exactly how much you want and are prepared to ask for.

The first step in determining how much money to ask for is to find out what the range of salaries is for your job at your office or firm. If you ask for an amount of money that is simply not offered for your position or skill level, you will not get far. Check with your human resources department to find out how much your company is willing to pay for your position.

It is possible that you are already close to the high end of your pay range. If this is the case, you will need to show what other companies pay people in your position so you will have information to bargain with. Make sure to check with businesses in your area. The same business in different cities may pay quite differently. The pay rates in New York City probably will not affect the rates of pay in Gary, Indiana.

Information on what other companies pay is not to be used as a threat, but merely as an example of the going rate for someone with your skills and experience. It is in a company's best interest to pay its employees similarly to other companies in its field. If your company is behind the times when it comes to pay, it may appreciate the chance to bring its pay rate up to speed.

The next step is to consider your own wants and needs. You will have to balance the answers to two questions: How much do you ideally want to make, and how much will you be willing to accept? Giving yourself a range will allow for room to bargain in case your employer is willing, but unable, to give you your highest request.

To help determine how much you want to make, ask yourself some further questions:

- Do you have specific goals that money will help you achieve?
- Have you budgeted out these goals?
- Are your goals reasonable, considering your pay range?
- In how much time do you want to achieve these goals?

- Will your lowest bid allow you to still move toward your goal?

Consider Alternatives

In addition to your ideal raise, you should also be prepared to discuss alternatives. Your company may honestly not be in a position to hand out more money on anyone's paycheck. Or it may be more advantageous to both you and your company to discuss alternative ways of increasing your pay. Non-pay benefits can be just as lucrative as actual money on your paycheck. For example, if you end up with more vacation time or a shorter work week without a change in pay, you will actually be getting paid more for working fewer hours. Additionally, unless your raise is large enough, it may not be enough to compensate for the taxes passed on it.

You should be familiar with the various types of alternative compensation measures. The following is a list of some of the common types of compensation. Become familiar with what companies offer. Decide whether any of these options work for you and your goals, and be prepared to discuss them as you negotiate your raise.

- **Flexible Spending Accounts (FSA):** With an FSA, an employee can have a certain amount of money withheld from his or her paycheck. This money can be used for predetermined expenses as set forth by the company's insurance and investment policies. The money is most commonly used for medical expenses, but is also sometimes used for dependant-related care.

- **401(k) plans:** With a 401(k), an employee can save for retirement while avoiding paying taxes on a portion of their income. The employee elects to have a percentage of his or her paycheck put into the plan. The company uses the money to invest, and the employee can recoup their investment upon retirement.

- **Insurance:** Most large companies will offer their employees a variety of medical, dental, property, auto, and life insurance. This allows the employee to feel taken care of in the event of an emergency, or simply to be able to attend to basic needs and care. Buying insurance in bulk allows the company to get the insurance for less than the average consumer would pay for it, and the employee does not have to shell out extra money for certain expenses.

- **Overtime:** Sometimes, especially when an employee is earning a salary instead of wages, working extra hours is just part of the package. This is to say that an employee on salary does not earn extra money for putting in extra hours. If you are a salaried employee who regularly works more than 40 hours a week, overtime — or extra pay for extra hours — can be a wonderful bonus.

If you work for wages, overtime can be a quick way to earn extra money. If an employee who earns wages works between 40 and 50 hours a week, those extra ten hours count as the first tier of overtime. That means that for those ten hours, the employee will earn time and a half instead of their regular hourly wage. In other words, if an employee earns $20 an hour, then for those extra ten hours, they will earn $30 an hour — their regular wage, plus half of their regular wage.

After those ten hours, or for work on the weekends, overtime can often be even higher. Because of this, many companies will restrict the amount of overtime employees can work. But if you are on wages and are willing to work extra hours, it may be possible to work out an arrangement to work extra hours at a higher rate.

- **Profit sharing:** A company may decide to contribute some of its profits to a fund that will be divided among employees who meet certain criteria. Employees who make more will often receive a larger portion of these profits, while employees who make less will receive a smaller portion.

- **Stock options:** Companies will sometimes allow employees to purchase stock in the company for reduced rates. This works well for the employee if the value of the stocks continues to rise. The employee gets the stock for an inexpensive rate while earning the money accrued as the stocks increase in value.

- **Free parking/ride sharing:** If you work in a major metropolitan area, parking rates can be at a premium. Many companies have arrangements with parking companies for reduced or free parking. See whether your company has this kind of a program.

Companies often receive tax benefits from going "green." This means if your company offers its employees access to public transportation for free or at a reduced cost, or if it sponsors programs where employees carpool, you may receive a benefit from the government.

Taking advantage of these kinds of programs can cut gas costs for you. It can also save on wear and tear on your car. While it may seem to be a minor amount, cutting small costs will add up over time and translate into more money that you get to keep each week.

- **Day care:** Day care is another expensive cost that your company may help you alleviate. If you have children, then you are aware of how expensive it can be to have someone take care of them while you are at work. According to a report by the National Association of Child Care Resource and Referral Agencies, day care can cost a family more than $10,000 a year.

  Some companies have on-site day-care facilities, or they may have arrangements with day-care providers in the area. Check with your human resources department to see whether your company provides any of these kinds of services.

- **Gym or social club membership:** Another popular perk that many businesses offer is to give their employees access to gyms or social clubs. Sometimes these memberships are offered at a reduced rate, and sometimes they are free.

  Whether the cost of membership is reduced or free, the membership is a benefit to both the company and the employee. Depending on the programs offered, a gym membership can run between a few dollars or more than $100 a month. Social club memberships can be even more expensive. By offering employees memberships to these types of facilities, companies give their employees a break while encouraging company loyalty and identity by getting employees together in one location, doing something fun.

- **Frequent flyer miles:** When companies pay for travel perks in bundles, they have access to cheaper rates. Sometimes, companies can pass along those perks to their employees through frequent flyer miles. An employee can accumulate these miles through hours worked and turn them in for discounts on travel.

- **Company discounts:** Companies may offer a variety of discounts at local and national businesses. These discounts can range from a percentage off the check at restaurants to special discounts on cell phone services with national carriers. Taking advantage of the discounts that your company offers can add up to considerable savings over time.

Putting it All Together

Organizing your information is as important as getting it in the first place. You will want to make sure you hand over this information as clearly and efficiently as possible. This will make things easier on your boss and make you look like a savvy, well-put-together business professional who definitely deserves the raise he or she is asking for.

Assemble your items like you would a report or presentation that you would give to a room full of clients. Although your boss may know you personally, this is not the time to pal around with him or her. Your raise is not about how well you two get along, but about how much you can bring to the company if they give you more money. Through your presentation, show them that you know how to woo clients, and you will woo yourself into a higher pay rate.

Enclose your presentation items in a presentation binder. These binders have a clear top cover and a solid back cover. This will keep your items neat and make it easy for your boss to quickly see your presentation among all the other things on his or her desk.

The first page should be your cover letter. Though you will be having a face-to-face meeting with your employer, you should still include a cover letter in your report. This will serve as your voice when you leave the office and your boss considers your raise. The cover letter should follow proper business format, as discussed earlier. The introductory paragraph should say you are asking for a raise and highlight the reasons why. The following paragraphs should explain those reasons in detail.

For example, your introductory paragraph could read something like this:

Dear Mrs. Walker,

During my five years at The Company, I have streamlined the billing file system and managed multiple successful projects, and I continue to meet and surpass expectations. My work shows that I am dedicated to the company and a strong employee. I would like to discus raising my salary from $45,300 a year to $47,500 a year. Following are examples of the work I have done, as well as what I hope to accomplish for the company after a raise.

Your letter should clearly state your intentions for a raise quickly. Do not beat around the bush and simply list your accomplishments and accolades. Being honest and upfront about why you have scheduled this meeting will make you look like a strong employee — the kind of employee whom employers want to reward with a raise.

In the letter, you should discuss achievements that set you apart from the pack. Do not compare yourself directly to other employees. Instead, state what you have done as objective events that showcase your work, talents, and drive. Be specific with what you have done and the executives and clients that your work involved. This way, your boss can easily cross-reference what you are talking about and know whom to contact to hear more good things about you.

Your concluding paragraph should let your boss know what else is in the presentation folder, remind him or her exactly what you are interested in, and thank them for their time and consideration.

> I have enclosed several items for your review. Enclosed, you will find letters of recommendation, a copy of my latest two performance reviews, and an explanation of my duties, showing how they have changed and increased in responsibility over time. Because of this information, I would ask that my salary be increased from $45,300 a year to $47,500 a year. Please let me know whether there is anything else I can provide. Thank you for your time and consideration.

Following the letter, you should include all supporting materials that you have collected. Each item should be free from errors, on clean paper, and bound so all the information is clear. When you put your presentation together this way, your boss will take notice.

To Review

You are in the home stretch now, and you have done considerable work to get to this point. Make sure you have the documentation and supporting materials to make your case as strong as possible.

- **Look at your latest performance review.** Whether there is positive information on it or areas in which you need to improve, the information is important. Continue to emphasize what your supervisor was pleased with, and make sure you are taking steps to correct what needed improvement.

- **Compare and contrast.** Find out what others in your position are making at other companies. You need to know what the pay trends are for your skills and expertise. If you are not making what new hires in your position are, then you are in a stronger position to justify your raise.

- **Recommendation letters.** Additional opinions from clients, co-workers, and executives will only strengthen the case you bring to your boss. Ask people you have worked for to write recommendation letters on your behalf. The letters should emphasize the work that you did for them and the benefits they received from the work.

- **Toot your own horn.** The journal that you keep of the work you do each day will help you create a list of accomplishments. You should be ready to speak about the good work you have done and be able to explain how your work had a positive effect on the office. So much the better if you had a particular award, either from your company or from a respected professional organization.

- **Show how you fit in.** By now, you should be well-aware of what your company wants in terms of finances and image. Creating a list explaining how you fit into those goals will help explain your case to your boss.

- **Know what you want.** Do not go into your boss's office without knowing exactly what you want in terms of a raise. It is not enough to know that you want "more" money; you should have an exact amount. Being strong and direct in asking for what you want will make you appear confident and assured. Not having a specific goal will weaken your case and may cause your boss to wonder whether you are always this indecisive when it comes to business decisions.

- **Do not shy away from alternatives.** There are other ways to add to your take-home pay. A variety of alternative methods of payment may be just as rewarding as actual money added on your check.

- **Put it together nicely.** By now, you will have collected a large number of documents, lists, and supporting material. Organize them in a way that will be easy for anyone to read through. Keeping your materials clearly organized will put you on the fast track to using them to convince your boss that you deserve your raise.

CASE STUDY: M. JANE MYERS

M. Jane Myers
Community volunteer
Newport, Tennessee

M. Jane Myers, a community volunteer who previously worked in administrative positions, emphasizes that when asking for a pay raise, you should never be too aggressive because, as she puts it, "An employer does not owe you any raise."

She believes dress plays an important role in asking for a pay raise or advancement within a company. "It is extremely important — anyone who does not take care of themselves will not take care of the organization," she said.

Any employee asking for a pay raise should have legitimate reasons, she noted. Among those reasons are an increase in workload and quality work performance, she said. If pay raises and reviews have not been discussed prior to employment, she believes an employee should work for the company at least six months before asking for a raise.

When meeting with a supervisor, she said the employee should not be too aggressive or have an attitude that is too disheartened. Good eye contact with the supervisor is also important, she added.

How to Not Get the Raise You Want...Ever

We have spent considerable time talking about the things you should do when pursuing a raise. However, there are some "don'ts" as well. While you want to be aggressive as you move toward your goals, you will want to avoid certain things. Employee raises are denied as often as they are rewarded. The following items will take you off of your boss's "good list" and keep your paycheck size from growing any time soon:

A bad sense of timing

As with asking someone out on a date, there is much to be said for timing when asking for a raise. You probably would not ask someone out just after he or she saw you do something embarrassing. The same idea should apply to asking your boss for a raise. If you have recently come out of a rough patch at work, you should probably wait until things are stable and calm before asking for your raise. Likewise, if the company itself is having serious trouble, you should probably hold off on your raise request until things have smoothed over. Asking for your raise while either you or your company is in hot water may come across as not being respectful of the current situation. Your employer will want to know that you have a good sense of timing in business. If you know when to approach about your raise, your boss may have more confidence in your ability to read other situations correctly.

An overly personal plea

It is quite possible that there are personal financial reasons why you want a raise. Maybe you are desperately trying to pay down some debt, or maybe you just want to take a luxurious vacation this year. But take care to remember that while these goals may top your priority list, they are not on your boss's priority list. Your boss is concerned with advancing company goals, so when you take your case to your boss, you should show that you are, too.

The truth is that everyone in the office probably wants more money. Your boss probably wants to make more money as well. Simply telling your employer that you want or need more money will not be enough of an argument. It is not that your boss will not understand your personal situation; it is simply a matter of being practical. If your boss awarded a raise to everyone who needed it for some personal reason, the company would likely soon go bankrupt.

Your raise meeting is not the time to let your boss know about your deepest, darkest secrets and desires. Your focus should be on how you contribute to the bottom line and how your raise will help you continue to add to the company's bottom line. Save the personal stories for your friends at a celebratory lunch or dinner.

Too many feelings

Just like your raise meeting is not the time to talk about personal goals, it is also not the time to talk about your feelings. Stick to the facts and to your presentation. Avoid getting ruffled by your boss's demeanor or comments. Even if you immediately hear good news, keep your emotions in check and stay professional. A smile and a handshake is an appropriate expression of pleasure — and displeasure. Respect your boss's position and professionalism, and save the temper tantrums for the comfort and safety of your own home.

Underhanded tactics

In prior chapters, it was discussed that one of the ways to increase your chances of getting a raise is to set yourself apart from your fellow employees. It was suggested that you do things like take on additional work, work more hours, and find problems to which you can provide solutions. But what you should never do is resort to less-than-ethical tactics, or sabotage anyone else's work.

When looking for problems to solve, it may be tempting to point out other employees. Avoid pointing fingers and, instead, shift the focus of the problem to a procedure or otherwise objective source of conflict. Tattling, name-calling, or gossiping to make yourself look better will only make you look worse in your employer's eyes. You will come across as though you are trying to make others look bad instead of trying to improve issues within the company. However, if you focus on procedural issues or company concerns, you will elevate your status and thus increase your chances of getting a raise.

Any problems that you do find should be genuine, actual problems. Do not create problems just so that you can solve them. Do not put any other employees in positions to make mistakes — do not set them up to fail so that you can look better. Everyone has to work in the office. Making things difficult for others will only make things difficult for you.

An entitled attitude

While, from an objective point of view, you have done the work that puts you in a good position to earn a raise, acting as though you are entitled to something will probably come across as arrogance and hurt your chances of getting your raise. Stay humble and appreciative, and you will put yourself in a stronger position to get the increase in your paycheck that you are looking for.

A presentation lacking research

You need to be prepared for anything that your boss may throw at you during your raise presentation. That means being aware of what others make in your position at other companies, the state of your own company, and your company goals and plans for the next few years. All these factors and more will figure into your boss's decision as to whether to give you a raise, so you need to be ready and able to speak to these things. Not being prepared will cast doubt on whether you are prepared for the rest of the work that you do.

You also need to be ready to talk in-depth about your own work. Your boss may have many questions about your recent job performance, and you will need to speak to all aspects of your work. He may ask how you came by the assignment, who worked on it with you, how long it took you to do the work, how long it normally takes to do the work, and what changes you enacted to make the work go more smoothly. Being able to speak to these issues capably and with confidence will make you stand out and put you in a good position to get your raise.

CASE STUDY: TAMMY C. SMITH

Tammy C. Smith
Technology & attendance facilitator
White Pine, Tennessee

Tammy C. Smith, technology and attendance facilitator for a county school system, says employers should always be aware of employees who are in need of a pay raise. "But if the employee has to go to the employer, they should be prepared to validate their request," she said. "Employers will have much more loyal and dedicated employees if they stay aware of people who deserve a raise and allocate as warranted."

Smith believes an increase in work load that was agreed upon when hired, and/or a job well-done, warrants a pay raise. "If your work load increases, or if you have not received a raise in a reasonable amount of time, it is the right time to ask for a raise. Also, if others in the same line of work are making significantly more wages, it is time to ask for a raise," she said.

She believes presenting documentation to an employer provides hands-on information when considering the request for a pay raise. "It can be used to show others who make the decision about advancement and raises who did not sit in on your one-on-one meeting," she added. "Things that should be included in your documentation are your work load, any conferences or classes you have attended to better accomplish your job, and especially, ways you have made your employer succeed above and beyond any goals set for the company."

PART III

Taking Your Case to Your Boss

All your work is useless if you do not conduct a good meeting with your boss. This section explains, in detail, how to explain to your boss that you are ready for a pay raise, and why you deserve one.

CHAPTER
12

Take Your Case to the Boss

By this point, you have done considerable work, and you are in the home stretch. You have evaluated yourself as an employee and worked to make yourself the best employee possible. You have collected supporting materials to justify your raise. All that is left is to present all this work to your boss. But there is still work involved. Approaching the meeting incorrectly can still sabotage your chance of getting a raise; do not let that work go to waste. The following section will discuss how to schedule, set, and conduct a strong, impressive meeting that wows your boss and gets you your raise.

CASE STUDY: ALONZO CUDD

Alonzo Cudd
Marketing consultant
Sherman Oaks, California

Alonzo Cudd, a marketing consultant, explained that before he got his first pay raise, he was hired as a marketing coordinator. He actually took a pay cut when he took the job. The company only did annual reviews, but he asked for a review within the first six months.

Six months later, Cudd reminded his boss that he was due for a review. She passed him along to the regional director, who flew down to discuss it with him. The regional director actually offered him a different job that came with more responsibilities. However, it did not come with a pay increase, so Cudd took the job and decided to petition for one.

"I called the regional director and told him that, based on the responsibilities of the new job, I should be paid a certain amount of money," he said. "He said that he wanted to see how I did at the job first." Cudd asked what the timeline was, and the director answered: three months. "So I asked him what he wanted to see over the next three months," said Cudd. " I asked him what I should try to achieve in that time, and I asked what those goals were. I knew that I could ask what he wanted from me and get a pretty direct answer."

One of the goals was to secure an entertainment or celebrity-driven event, and he had to increase the sales for two of his stores by a certain percentage. The regional director also wanted Cudd to help another employee create a program that introduced the company's product to its clients.

"I thought the goals were really reasonable goals," he said. "But they were still challenging, so I didn't feel like they were just trying to find a way to put me off."

Cudd finished his goals before the three months passed, but waited until the three-month date passed to let his boss know.

"He didn't tell me to do this, but I did it: Every time I made progress on a certain goal, I would update my direct boss and the regional director," he said. "I would talk directly to my boss about the steps I was taking toward these goals. Both my boss and the regional director would give feedback along the way."

After three months, he contacted his boss and updated him about his success at meeting the goals. He reminded her that his raise was to be discussed at that

CASE STUDY: ALONZO CUDD

time. A few weeks later, he received a pay raise. However, Cudd was denied an increase in his yearly bonus.

After being denied the bonus increase, he asked why he was not allowed to have it. It came down to a budget issue at the top levels of the company; there was not enough money in that year's budget to give him a bonus.

Cudd brought the issue up at his next review. He said he thought it was important to let them know that he did want the bonus, because if they did not know that he was expecting an increase, they would not have thought to budget it for the next year. After the review, he got the bonus increase.

Make an Appointment

Obviously, you will need to set a specific date and time to sit down with your boss and discuss your raise. Even if you work in a casual office environment where employees are welcome to chat with the boss at any time, you will want quiet, focused time with your boss, so set an appointment. If your boss is able to clear some time off of his or her schedule for you, you can be sure you will have his or her full attention and a better chance at making a strong case for your raise.

Contact your supervisor's assistant and find out when the best time for this kind of meeting is. Do not let yourself be assigned an appointment time that is not advantageous to you. Ask what time of day your boss prefers to meet. Is he or she a morning person, or does he or she prefer to handle these kinds of things at the end of the day? Avoid getting scheduled in the middle of an already busy day. You want your boss to be as open and amenable as possible to your request, so try to find a time when there is not too much else going on. Of course, you do not want to bully your way into a time slot, but work with the person who handles the schedule of your boss to find a time that is free from other distractions and stresses.

CASE STUDY: TABITHA E. JENKINS

Tabitha E. Jenkins
Office manager
Jonesborough, Tennessee

Tabitha E. Jenkins, office manager for an emergency medical service, said she expects an employee to act professional and have a good work ethic. She also points out that appearance plays an important role.

"You do not want to reward someone if they do not look like they need to be rewarded," she said.

"Being on time, being professional in appearance, having appropriate behavior, and knowing the 'ins and outs' of the job that an employee does is what I expect from an employee who is requesting a pay raise."

Jenkins thinks an employee should work for a company between six months and one year before requesting a pay raise.

She says organizational skills are also important: "You do not want to give a position to someone who does not know how to keep order," she said. "And do not chew gum, do not arrive late, and do not arrive half-ready for the meeting."

Control the Meeting

Though your employer is the one in charge, this meeting is one time when you do not want him or her to be. Since you are there to get something that you want, you will need to make sure you control the tone, pace, and focus of the meeting so that you achieve the outcome you are working toward.

Have an agenda before you come to the meeting. It is not enough to say to yourself "I want to talk about a raise." You will need to take your boss through the logic that proves that you deserve a raise.

Start with establishing a rapport with your boss. Do not barge in, immediately demanding money. Instead, use the usual small talk to your advantage. Asking "How are you today?" does not have to be an insincere question. Instead, listen to what your boss has to say. Showing that you are genuinely interested in what he or she has to say will make your presence more meaningful. Making a personal connection in the first few minutes of your meeting will make your professional connection that much stronger.

Move into small talk about the company. Ask about recent goings-on or recent good fortune that the company has had. Make it clear that you are a part of those activities. By saying something like, "We really had a good presentation for the Sanchez account. I would imagine that we will be signing them for another year soon," you insert yourself into company life and associate yourself with something positive — two things that your boss will want to know you can do when considering your raise.

Now you should move into talking about the purpose of the meeting. Remember to keep it positive. Remind your boss that you like your job and are simply looking to take the next logical step.

For example:

> "Thank you for taking my meeting today. As you know, I have been with The Company for five years, and I have really enjoyed it. I have felt challenged and excited by the work, and my track record shows that I have successfully risen to those challenges. In fact, I had several strong comments on my latest performance review, and I wanted to take some time to discuss my compensation package. I would like to review some things that I think will show how I have grown as an employee. And I have put together some materials that show good things for the company."

Make sure that, in addition to an extra copy of your supporting materials for yourself, you also write out your agenda and have it with you during the meeting. This will ensure that you remember to discuss everything that you need to. Your agenda should list your specific goals and the supporting materials you have provided for your boss. The meeting will be your chance to discuss the supporting materials in detail.

Focus on a few major accomplishments, rather than bombarding your boss with every good thing you have done since being hired. Select the accomplishments that most clearly demonstrate how you can help the company. When you discuss them, give your boss all the details he or she will need to see the situation clearly. Do not assume your boss will immediately understand the nuances of what you have done. Give the background of the situation, what you did to affect a change, and how that change helped the company.

Remember to be honest. Your boss will be looking at your work carefully, so this is not the time to inflate what you have done. If you have done the work outlined in the first part of this book, by now you will likely have plenty of accolades to discuss. Resist the urge to fudge facts to make your case stronger. If your boss finds out that you have not been totally honest, your entire case will be weakened, and your raise will likely disappear.

Show your boss that you have done your research. Mention what others are making in the field at this time. As was discussed earlier, the pay for certain jobs may change radically from year to year. Make sure your boss knows your skills are valuable. Compare this to your current compensation package.

Before you tell your boss what increases you want, let them know you are thinking about the company. Tell your boss about your goals for the following year. This will let them know you can focus on the company. It also gives your boss something to look forward to. Explain how your goals go above and beyond what you are currently doing. In other words, your goals should not be to merely continue your excellent level of work; your goals should include something new for the company — something that will bring them more money and prestige.

Next, state what you would like in your proposed compensation package. Be detailed and specific. It is not enough to say that you want "more" money. Rather, give your boss a specific salary that you would like to receive. Frame your pay goals in terms of how it relates to others in your field — not in your office — and how it will help you achieve your professional goals.

Finally, summarize the high points of your meeting. Remind your boss that you have not just come in asking for more money; rather, you have shown him or her that you are a valuable employee with a strong future at this company. You want to be there, and your track record shows that you will be a valuable asset at the company for years to come.

Keep Confident

If you are not used to setting the agenda for and controlling a meeting, it can feel intimidating. But approaching the meeting with confidence is crucial to getting what you want out of it. If you go in unsure of yourself or without the proper preparation, your boss will not be swayed to your argument. If you do not have confidence in what you are saying, why should anyone else?

The first step in showing confidence is to believe in what you are saying. You can learn to do this by backing it up with facts, research, and preparation. And because you have done so much work to this point, there is no reason why you should not believe in what you are saying. If you have followed the steps in this book, you will either have become an excellent employee, or strengthened already-strong skills and become an exceptional employee. Either way, there is no reason why you should not feel comfortable and confident with your work at this point.

The next step toward feeling more confident in this, or in any presentation you make, is to remember that your audience wants you to do well. There are few situations more uncomfortable or unpleasant than watching an actor on stage in a live performance who does not know his lines, or who has let stage fright overcome him. We have all been bored by shy public speakers who deliver dry, uninteresting addresses. Audiences want speakers to do well.

Because your boss is in a position of power, and because you are ultimately at his or her disposal, you may feel that he or she is hoping you fail. This is likely not the case. At worst, your boss is hoping you do not deliver a flawed, uncomfortable presentation; at best, your boss is looking forward to rewarding you for a job well-done. Your boss wants to hear good things about his or her company and his or her employees. Your boss wants you to do well during this meeting, and so do you. You should feel confident that you and your boss have the same goals. You are starting the meeting in agreement, so there is no reason to expect that you cannot end the meeting in agreement as well.

The final step in feeling confident is to keep your eye on your goal. Remember, you have set this meeting for an important purpose. Think about how good you will feel about your job and about yourself if you achieve that goal.

Despite the above information, keeping confident can still be a difficult task. If you find your confidence waning during your meeting, simply take a deep breath and remember what you have read to this point. Try smiling or the age-old trick of reminding yourself of something pleasant or funny. These actions can create a break in the tension, stop your mind from stressing, and get you back to feeling calm, collected, and confident.

Use Effective, Persuasive Language

While much of communication is non-verbal, the most obvious part of communication is about the words we use and how we use them. Salespeople have been using effective, persuasive tactics to convince patrons to buy products for as long as there have been products to buy. Commercials, billboards, and even news reports use language to keep their audiences engaged in what they are saying. Learning to use language in the right way can help you keep your boss engaged and get you closer to the raise you have been working toward.

Powerful words

There are a handful of words in the English language that advertisers frequently use to catch the attention of consumers and direct buyers toward their products. It is not an accident that the same familiar words show up repeatedly on packaging, in commercials, painted on billboards, and in the pages of marketing materials. These words are powerful, evocative, and effective. If you use them throughout your raise presentation, you will have the same effect on your boss that good advertisements have on consumers. Advertisers hope that you will buy what they are selling, and with the right vocabulary, your boss will be more likely to buy what you are selling.

Verbs

Verbs are powerful words to use when trying to get and keep someone's attention and convince them of a position. Verbs indicate action and movement, and in the business world, action and movement are paramount. Your employer does not want to feel like he or she is standing still at the company. He or she will want to feel like his or her team is on the move, is making changes, and is affecting the company in an active way. Using verbs in your presentation will help evoke this feeling.

When deciding what to say to your boss during your raise presentation, try following the advice of Leo Burnett. Burnett was an advertising executive who came up with many recognizable icons used to advertise and brand products. Some of these include The Jolly Green Giant, The Marlboro® Man, and Tony the Tiger®. Burnett conducted extensive research on some of the most powerful speeches delivered and ad campaigns run. He found that the more powerful pieces of communication had considerably more verbs than adjectives.

When you prepare your raise presentation, avoid simply listing attributes associated with your work. Saying that your work was "good" or "strong" is fine, but you should also make sure to not only describe the merit of the work, but detail the work in terms of what actions you actually took.

For example, instead of saying, "My reorganization of the office was effective," say what you actually did. The rewrite of that sentiment might look something like this: "After I completed the Thompson account, I recognized that our backup files were often lost. So I created a filing system for closed accounts. I moved our old records to a more convenient facility and updated the existing records for accounts that are near closure."

Notice how much more effective the second way of stating the accomplishment of "reorganizing" was. Both statements could be true, but the second is more evocative. It lets the person hearing this information know exactly what was done. It nearly paints a picture of what the new office situation looks like. It will be easy for the person hearing this information to visualize not only the work, but how the office benefited from it.

Adjectives and adverbs

The above is not to say that your work should be devoid of adjectives and adverbs — words that describe nouns and verbs, respectively. Just like strong verb placement does, adjectives and adverbs help paint a complete picture of what a speaker is describing. Think about a restaurant menu: "Salmon, potatoes, and greens" does not sound nearly as enticing as "Fresh Atlantic salmon served with creamy, home-style mashed potatoes and perfectly seasoned greens." The second menu listing helps you get an idea of what is being served; you can almost taste it. Reading that description may even cause a physical reaction — such as a stomach growl or a watering in the mouth — as you read. The goal with using adjectives and adverbs is to use the ones that are most evocative in your situation — and most important to a businessperson's ears.

You will want to use adjectives and adverbs that indicate growth and development. People in business are first and foremost concerned with increasing their business. They want to know that their work is having an effect on the company and that the company is growing because of it. This is important, so make sure your raise presentation makes it clear that you have been and will be a part of the company's growth. Some examples of words that indicate progress follow:

- **Better.** If something you did is better than what came before it, then it will be clear you are causing progress to happen. Ideally, by now you can say that the filing system you created led to better organization, or that the phone script you wrote led to better customer service. While preparing for your raise, something you have done should have caused something to work better, people to feel better, or the company to look better.

- **Successfully.** Who can complain about work that is done successfully? Combining the word successfully with a verb explaining what you did, as in, "I identified a problem with our customer service procedure and successfully enacted a solution," should make your boss's ears perk up. Your boss will want to know not only that you took on additional work, but that you completed it and did it well. Taking on extra work or identifying problems is only part of what you should be doing; you should also be able to do the extra work well.

- **Efficient.** Companies are always looking to do more with less, such as increasing profit by making the same number of widgets for less money. Companies do not want their employees to spend extra time doing work if it is not necessary. Let your boss know not only that you did something, but also that you did it efficiently. Look at it from your boss's point of view. If you reorganized the filing system, but it made the filing system more complicated and convoluted, causing employees to spend more time figuring it out, then you did not do something that the company would value. But if you can let your boss know that what you did caused less time to be spent on any one task, then you have something there that your company can appreciate.

- **Creative.** Regardless of how mundane some of the work you have to do each day can be, your boss will want to know that you are not an automaton doing things without thinking about them. He or she will want to know that you can exercise creativity when solving problems. Letting your boss know you approached a situation creatively or found a creative solution to a client's issues will let him or her know that you can think in interesting ways that will likely benefit the company in the future.

- **Innovative.** Your boss will want to know that your ideas are not only unique, but that they are also progressive — that your ideas reflect current trends in business. Letting your employer know that a solution you developed to a problem was innovative should catch your employer's attention. Businesses need to change with the times to grow. Using this adjective as you describe your accomplishments will help your employer see you as someone who can take the business into the future.

Words and phrases that assume agreement

Ultimately, your goal in this presentation is to cause your boss to agree with your justification for deserving a raise — and then to give it to you. The first part of that is that your boss has to agree with you. Instead of starting things off defensively, start from a position where you assume that your boss does agree with you. The power of suggestion is powerful. And when you use it to imply that your boss agrees with you, you will put yourself much closer to getting your raise.

To imply agreement, simply add "don't you?" "right?" or "doesn't it?" to the end of sentences and questions. For example, you might say something like, "The company is looking to add more customers at the lower end of its demographic during the next fiscal year, right? Well, it makes sense to put an employee who is a part of that demographic on that team, does it not?" By adding these simple tags to ideas that you want your boss to agree with, you will subtly imply that they do already or should agree with you.

Be careful with your attitude while you do this. You do not want to come across as patronizing or arrogant. You also do not want to try and get your employer to agree with facts that are not true, so make sure your research backs up what you want your boss to agree with.

CASE STUDY: BRAD BELL

Brad Bell
Entertainment entrepreneur
Los Angeles, California

Brad Bell, an entertainment entrepreneur, has worked in sales and found that the same tactics that work in sales also work in business situations.

"When you are dealing with a client or manager and you are trying to get something from them, whether it is a raise or anything else, you need to be able to close them. Using leading language and language based on the way a person processes information — what I call sensory communication — can help you close anything," he said.

"I have been inspired by everyone from Napoleon Hill to Tony Robbins to Zig Ziglar to any of the infamous and endlessly quoted authors of affirmation. I have

CASE STUDY: BRAD BELL

used many pieces of their advice to form my own tactics and find the following to be particularly helpful," said Bell.

"When a person talks slower and looks to the left or to the right when they talk, they tend to be an auditory person. They tend to take all their information in by listening. When a person looks up and talks faster, they tend to be visual. When people look down and talk more slowly, that person tends to be kinesthetic in the way they take in information — they go on how they feel," he said.

"In sales, you'll talk to these people differently. It works in business, too. If you are talking to someone who appears to be an auditory person, say something like this to them during your presentation: 'Listen to this. I closed more clients than anyone else on my team last quarter.' If you are talking to a visual person, try saying something like 'Look at these numbers. They show that I had the highest closure rate of anyone on the team.' And if you are talking to a feeling person, you might say something like 'I really feel like these numbers make it clear that I out-closed the rest of the team.'"

According to Bell, everybody tunes in and out during conversation. To keep their attention, you have to study them to figure out how they take in information. Using key words based on the way people take in information, like "look," "listen," and "feel," will help you get their attention and focus it back on you. You do not say it aggressively, but when you say these words, it subconsciously triggers something in them that causes them to pay more attention to you than they were.

"I've found that it's especially effective when you follow those key words with 'here's the thing,' or 'here's how it is.' Lowering your voice a little also helps. It's like walking into a room and taking a deep breath in front of a microphone. It gets everyone ready to listen to you," he said.

"From every great success story, to every temporary sales gig, to every human interaction we have, we are always selling ourselves," Bell said. "We are always trying to work our way up, whether we know it or not."

Respect the Relationship

Tailor the tone of your meeting to match the relationship you have with your boss. If you are generally friendly with each other, feel free to let that tone continue through to this meeting. However, if you have a more formal relationship, this meeting is not the time to make your boss your best bud.

Being too casual or speaking with too much familiarity to a boss with whom you have a formal relationship can make you come across as insincere or pushy. Likewise, being too formal with a boss with whom you have a friendly relationship with could also make you look insincere.

That being said, even if you have a friendly relationship with your boss, you should not speak to them like you do during a casual lunch. You want to respect your boss's authority. You also want to look like a confident businessperson. Friendly or not, your boss will not be evaluating you simply on how chummy you are in the meeting. Your boss will be looking at you as a businessperson. He or she will be deciding how well you fit into the corporate structure. To look like you fit in, you will need to present yourself professionally.

Keep it brief

Do not take up too much of your boss's time with this meeting. Though you want to make sure you get out all the information that will support your case, you do not want to be there too long. Talking more will not make your case stronger; the facts you present to your boss will make your case stronger, as will giving a quick, efficient, and fact-filled presentation. Keeping the meeting brief and to the point will be more effective in proving why you deserve to be seen as a savvy, capable business person.

Use leading statements and questions

When you sit down with your boss to discuss your raise, you will want to make sure you keep the conversation on track. You are there for one specific purpose. Do not allow yourself to become distracted with small talk or discussion of other business. There will be plenty of time to talk about these things after you get your raise.

The way you phrase what you say during this meeting is one of the strongest tools you have to make sure the meeting goes the way you want it to. We have already discussed how the specific words that you use can change the way that you are perceived. The right words have power, and the right phrasing of those words has even more power. You do not have to be aggressive, cold, or mean when you meet with your boss. But if you confidently use certain conversation techniques, you will make your case even stronger.

The first thing you should take care to do when you speak with your boss about your raise is to avoid asking yes-or-no questions. While getting a "yes" answer from a question like, "Do you like the work I did on the last account?" may seem positive, you will ultimately want much more than a simple answer. You want to know specifics so you can play to them. It is not enough to know your boss likes your work; to make a strong case for your raise, you need to know what your boss likes about your work. That way, you can emphasize what your boss sees as your strong points — making your case for your raise even stronger.

Questions are a good way to check in with your boss, to keep him or her involved in the conversation, to take stock of your progress, and to keep the conversation going. Do not shy away from asking them. Instead, rephrase the way you ask them to prevent yourself from asking easily dismissible yes or no questions. Open-ended questions will do a good job of facilitating discussion.

Do not ask, "Do you think that I am doing a good job with the new account?" It makes sense to ask a question like that to ascertain what your employer thinks of you. But a yes-or-no question can too easily illicit a simple negation of your question — or an insincere "yes."

Instead, take control with your questions. To find out more clearly what your employer thinks, ask, "What do you think about the changes we made in the new account?" This will lead your employer to answer you with a complete answer that gives you insight into what he or she finds important. Take note of what your employer says. Use the positive comments to highlight other similar work that you have done. Use any criticism as an opportunity to improve.

Another way of moving the conversation in the direction you want it to go is to use leading statements. Leading statements work like leading questions, only they lead to discussion and do not open the floor for your boss to answer a question. Leading statements can be extremely effective in keeping the conversation moving. The more effectively you move the conversation forward, the sooner you will get your raise.

A leading statement is like the topic statement of a paragraph. It will let your boss know what you will be discussing next. Instead of asking your boss what he or she thinks about the new account, you can lead your boss into a positive frame of reference for the next topic of discussion. For example, a statement like this can be a strong addition to your conversation: "I would like to discuss some of the positive changes we have made to the new account." A statement like this frames the next part of the conversation and puts you in control of it.

Body Language

Experts believe that more than 50 percent of communication is non-verbal. That means that more than half of what anyone gleans from what you say has nothing to do with the words that you use. Learn to use body language effectively, and you will put yourself in a good position to convince your boss that you deserve a raise.

One way to make sure your conversation is as effective as you want it to be is to use body language to your advantage. You can communicate just as much, if not more, with the way you hold your hands, control your eye contact, and even position your chair in your boss's office than you can with what you say. Your words and your presentation are only part of the battle. To get your raise, make sure you are using all the tools at your disposal.

Another interesting trait about body language is that your mind can lead your body or your body can lead your mind. More often than not, body language exposes our inner thoughts and feelings. But if you learn to control your movements, you can make this concept work the other way around. If you begin to practice positive body language, regardless of how you are feeling or what you are thinking, your body will lead your mind toward thinking more positively — making you a more effective communicator and happier in general.

Nod and your boss will nod with you

Experts believe that the head nod evolved from a formal bow. It is a move that symbolizes agreement and good feelings. The nod can also be seen as a submissive move that indicates that the person nodding is willing to go along with what the other person in a conversation is saying. Even people who are born without their sense of sight will begin to nod when they want to say "yes." This shows just how innate and powerful nodding your head can be. Learning to use it to your advantage will help you when you meet with your boss.

It is not just the nod itself, but also the speed of the nod that communicates clearly. Quick nods of the head can indicate impatience; it can make the recipient of the nod feel the need to hurry their conversation. A slow nod, however, can show that the listener is genuinely interested in what the other person is saying. Take care to notice how you nod and what it may be communicating to your boss. Nod too quickly when your boss is speaking, and you may give the indication that you are not listening to his or her input. But if you nod slowly, you will be showing respect and concern for what your boss has to say.

A slow, thoughtful head nod will also encourage your boss to agree with you. Like a yawn in a crowded room, if you start nodding, your boss will likely start nodding with you. Use this tactic to your advantage. Adding a nod when you give part of your pitch will encourage your boss to nod with you, and then agree with you.

For example, do not just say, "We made some good progress with the Mitchell account." Instead, start nodding your head when you get to the good news that you are about to deliver. This will lead your boss to agree with you before you even get to the end of the sentence.

What to do with your hands

If the eyes are the windows to the soul, hand gestures can be seen as windows to your thoughts. Your hands can reveal if you are excited, nervous, aggressive, or lying. Therefore, it is important to take care with what you are doing with your hands.

- **Hands folded with interlocked fingers:** If you are trying to control your nerves or appear professional, folding your hands with your fingers through each other may seem like the best choice. It looks neat, it keeps your hands still, and it seems like a neutral position. But this is actually not what you will be communicating with this hand position. Experts agree that this hand position signals an attempt to hide frustration; it tends to show that someone is holding back a negative attitude. Using this in front of your boss may actually make you seem tense and uptight. Instead, unclench your hands so that you can use them freely during your discussion.

- **Open palms:** Children will often put their hands behind their backs when they are telling lies. Consequently, keeping your palms open and facing the person to whom you are talking is a sign that you are being honest. Open palms also indicate that you are open to hearing what your boss has to say. An upturned, open palm is also a sign that you are non-threatening. This is in contrast to a down-turned palm, which indicates an attempt to exert control and authority. Keep your palms in an open position, especially when you are touting your achievements in the office, and you will earn your boss's trust.

- **Finger pointing:** The single pointed finger can be a real turn-off for anyone who is listening. Experts agree that the pointed finger is aggressive and can make a listening audience feel defensive. If you regularly use this hand gesture, you will need to take care to avoid it. There is a quick fix to the finger point that can take you from looking aggressive to looking calm and focused. Bring your pointing finger down into an "OK" position — where the index finger makes a circle with the thumb. You can also flatten out the circle in the "OK" position. Any way that you can bring your pointing finger in will change the aggressive finger point to a hand position that shows you are confident in what you are saying, instead of trying to bully your point across.

- **Crossed arms:** Crossing your arms over your body will not have a positive effect on your meeting. It will make you look defensive at worst, insecure at best. Fully crossing both your arms over your chest is an aggressive gesture. It shows you are not interested in what is being said and you are more interested in protecting yourself and your position than you are in engaging in a conversation. Crossing one of your arms over yourself is a childlike gesture that reeks of insecurity. Children will hug themselves when they feel upset or threatened. Women tend to demonstrate this gesture by holding one arm with the other. Men tend to exhibit this same gesture by holding one hand with the other and letting them hang in front of the front of their pants. Either way, this is not a gesture that instills faith in the stance you are taking. You definitely do not want to make your boss see you as an unconfident in what you are saying. So take care to keep your arms off your body.

- **Nervous tics:** There are many small movements that add up to one big idea: You are nervous. While it may be nice to find things to do with your hands, the wrong movements will weaken your presentation. Some of these include playing with sleeves and cufflinks, picking lint off of your clothes, and holding paper, pens, and cups in front of your body. Take care to notice if you do these things. Stopping yourself from doing them will make you seem more confident and make your boss more confident in giving you a raise.

Give your bosses a mirror
and they will like what they see

Another good way to establish rapport with those you are talking to is to mirror what they do with their body. This means that if they lean forward, you lean forward. If they cross their legs one way, you do the same. Mirroring is a powerful tool you can use to help your boss see you as an employee who is worth rewarding with a raise.

Mirroring happens naturally among friends and partners. Have you ever noticed how people who have been married for a long time seem to be similar in their mannerisms? They talk, walk, laugh, and maybe even dress similarly. This is because when people like one another, they will naturally — and unconsciously — try to be more like each other. Taking the same physical stance that your boss does is a silent but strong way of telling your boss that you like and want to be like him or her. Seeing her- or himself reflected in your body posture will make your boss feel more at ease.

You should also listen to your boss's tone of voice and rate of speech. If your boss speaks quickly, you should, too. If he or she speaks more slowly and deliberately, you should as well. Do not imitate your boss; this is not a chance to try out a comedy routine at his or her expense. Respectfully mirroring his or her tone and speed will build rapport and get the two of you into a natural rhythm that makes conversation easy and comfortable.

A good, firm shake

A solid handshake before a meeting is like a good appetizer before a meal. It lets your meeting partner know you are sure of yourself and ready for the meeting that is about to take place.

Your handshake should be firm, but not painfully strong. A weak handshake is uncomfortable for the other person and does nothing to instill confidence. It feels as though you are unsure or scared of the meeting.

You should shake at a comfortable distance. Coming in too close will make many people uncomfortable and make you seem more aggressive than you would like. Also, avoid pushing your arm out when you shake. This will indicate you are trying to keep your meeting partner away from you.

Smile sincerely

Smiles are always welcome, especially in situations that can be tense, like a business meeting. You may be tempted to put on your "game face" and not show a jovial attitude with a smile. But a smile is a powerful tool. It shows you are open to the other person in the room, and like a yawn or other forms of body language, smiles can be contagious.

Take care to smile with a genuine, sincere smile. A fake smile is as powerful as a real one, just in the other direction. A sincere smile not only activates the muscles around the mouth, but also the muscles around the eyes and the side of the face. In a sincere smile, the eyes will squint and the face will pull back. This leads to "smile lines," which we unfortunately associate with age. But the lines created from a warm and genuine smile are a welcome addition to your face during a meeting.

An insincere smile looks the same at first blush, but there is a difference. A fake smile — the kind you might give for a stiffly posed photograph — engages only your mouth. The muscles around the eyes and the side of the face will remain relatively still.

You may not consciously recognize a fake smile, but it will have an effect on you, and more importantly, on your boss. He or she may not know why he or she does not trust everything you say, but the feeling will be there. A fake smile can show that the person smiling is afraid or intimidated. It can also communicate disinterest, insincerity, or distraction. None of these are ideas that you want your face to communicate. You do not have to grin from ear-to-ear — too much smiling can be a put-off as much as not smiling at all. Rather, you should have a pleasant, friendly smile that comes naturally as you speak.

If you have a hard time relaxing enough around your boss to smile, or if you simply do not like this person enough to smile at him or her, you will need to find something to smile about so your meeting can give you the outcome you are looking for. Before your meeting, think about the things that you do like about your employer. Maybe he or she is good at his or her job, and you admire that. Or he or she may have told a good joke recently that made you chuckle. Try smiling about that. If you cannot find anything about your boss to smile about, try finding something in your office that you like — a nice plant or a picture — and smile at that. Or think about how happy you will be when you get your raise, and smile about that.

Practice

Some of these bodily movements may come easily to you; others may not. You should observe yourself in a mirror to see how you look when you speak. It is possible that you are reading your own body language completely incorrectly, and you are not aware of what you are silently communicating.

Go through your presentation with your boss and determine where the important sections are. Select a few key points where it will be crucial that your boss agrees with you. For example, when you list your accomplishments, discuss how they positively affected the company. This will be an important point, and you will need your boss's agreement. Therefore, you should employ some of the agreement-creating moves as you speak.

You should also practice these moves during your daily routine. Every time you interact with another person is a chance to positively influence the discussion with your body language. Practicing effective body language throughout your day will give you the confidence to use it effectively when you meet with your boss.

If you discover you regularly use negative body language such as sitting with your arms crossed or pointing when you speak, you may feel defensive about changing it. You might simply feel more "comfortable" with how you express yourself non-verbally. You may also be tempted to say that you do not mean anything negative by the way you hold yourself. But to communicate effectively, you must be aware of how others may interpret what you are doing. Practicing non-verbal cues that encourage agreement and positive feelings will make you a better communicator and get you that much closer to getting your raise.

Body language to avoid

Your boss may not have the luxury of having read this or other primers on body language. It is possible that your boss will have no idea just how much information your body is revealing. However, your boss — like all people — will pick up on the most negative aspects of body language. It may be unconscious, and your boss may not be able to tell you exactly why he or she was put off by your demeanor.

There are a few body positions that you should avoid at all costs. These are:

- Clenched fists
- Crossed arms
- Hands covering the mouth

Avoiding these positions will make you look and feel more confident, and when you look confident, your boss will be more apt to respond positively to you and your requests.

Read your boss's body language

When you sit down and meet with your boss, you should not just mind your own body language; you should also pay attention to the way your boss holds his or her body. Checking in with your boss's body language will let you know whether your message is getting through. If your boss is responding to you with positive body language, you will know you are on the right track. However, if you are getting resistant or negative body language, that should be a clue to change your tactics. Either way, it is important for good business communication to be able to interpret the body language of others.

We will start at the top and work our way down.

The eyes

When people are happy or excited, their pupils will dilate. Unlike when the optometrist forces your pupils to dilate during an exam, a natural dilation is a good sign. Consider that in literature, villains are often described as "beady-eyed," while writers will often describe the heroine or love interest as "doe-eyed" — conjuring images of big eyes that are wide open. People like the idea of wide open eyes because of the positive connotations.

You should be making eye contact as you speak, but do not just stare into your boss's eyes; take note of what you see there. If the pupils are wide open, you are doing well, and your boss is pleased with that you are saying. If the pupils are small, your boss may not be angry with you, but you may not be swaying him or her to your side just yet.

The mouth

The size and shape of the smile and the lines around the mouth are strong indicators of feeling. Learn to read them correctly, and you will be able to know more than what your boss is directly saying to you.

A smile is the most obvious indicator of happiness; however, the particulars of any smile are important to recognize. As we discussed earlier, a genuine smile involves the muscles of the eyes and the side of the face as well as the mouth. So if your boss is smiling, note the lines around the eyes and the side of the face as well. If they are present, you are getting a genuine smile, and you are on the right track. If not, you may need to reconsider what you are doing to encourage a genuine smile.

The lower jaw also tells you much what the smiling person is thinking. A sincere smile will slightly engage the lower jaw, and it may drop a bit. However, if the jaw is dropped too much, this may be a sign that the smiling person is trying too hard to make it look as though he or she agrees. An overly dropped lower jaw may come along with an insincere smile. If you see this sign, you may be on the wrong track.

Closed lips on your boss's face do not necessarily mean the two of you are not in agreement. But even without a smile, you can tell how happy your boss is. Closed lips are not the same as pursed lips. Lips that are closed, but relaxed, may indicate focus — your boss is listening and paying attention to what you are saying. However, if your boss's lips are pressed together tightly, he or she may be holding in negative feelings.

The arms and hands

Just like your own arms and hands will indicate how you feel about what you are saying, your boss's arms and hands will also indicate how he or she feels about what you are saying. Because people do not typically "listen" with their hands the way that they "talk" with their hands, you will most likely be observing your boss's hands at rest. However, still hands can communicate even when they are not moving.

One position you may see your boss's hands adopt is the "steeple." In the steeple, the fingertips are together and the palms are close to each other. Sometimes the hands will rock back and forth while the fingertips keep touching. People who are in a superior position will often use this hand position when speaking to someone who is in a lower position than they are.

The steeple signifies confidence and could mean your boss is either confident in you or confident in what they are about to say to you. If there are other positive gestures associated with this hand position, such as a smile or wide pupils, you can feel confident that you are in a good position. However, if the steeple follows negative body language, such as a frown or crossed arms, you may want to re-evaluate what it is you are saying at that moment.

If your boss's arms are crossed, notice exactly how they are crossed. There are slight variations that mean slightly different things. Take care to notice these differences, and you will have a better chance at correctly interpreting what your boss may be thinking about you and your presentation.

If the arms are crossed in front of the chest, this may be an attempt to create a barrier between the two of you. This could be due to any number of reasons. But whatever the reason, this is generally not a positive sign. Likewise, if your boss's hands are clenched while the arms are crossed, this is definitely not a good sign.

A thumbs-up should be seen as a welcome sign. If your boss's arms are crossed but the thumbs are visible, this is a positive sign. It likely means that while your boss is still trying to keep some distance between the two of you, he or she is not totally closed off to your ideas. Also, if this position comes toward the end of your meeting and is accompanied with other positive body movement, keep up what you are doing, because you are doing well.

The legs and feet

The legs and feet are an important way to know what someone may be thinking. People tend to be aware of what the look on their face may be or what they are doing with their hands. The lower half of the body, however, is often forgotten. But that does not mean the legs and feet do not have things to say. And if you are aware of what your boss's legs and feet are doing, you will be in a good position to determine what your boss thinks about what you are saying.

One leg lightly crossed over the other is a typical and comfortable sitting position. If your boss is sitting in this position, you can rest assured that things are fine. However, if crossed arms accompany the crossed legs, it is likely that your boss has withdrawn from the conversation and is not giving you the attention you would like.

A variation of the leg cross can occur when the ankle of one leg rests on the knee of the other leg. This position signifies that the sitter feels — or would like to feel — that they are in a position of dominance. The hands on the crossed leg signify an even more obstinate, stubborn mindset. Because of this emotional connection to this position, you may have a difficult time convincing your boss of your point. You will have a better chance of bringing your boss to agree with you if both feet are on the floor.

If both feet are on the floor, take a look at your boss's ankles. The meaning of the position of the ankles is similar to the meaning of hand positions. When the ankles are apart and resting on the floor, you can translate this the way you would open hands. It signifies that the listener is open to what you are saying and feeling positive about it. However, if the ankles are crossed, the listener could be holding back negative feelings. It is similar to clenched hands or pursed lips. It may symbolize frustration or tension. If your boss's ankles are in this position, you will need to re-evaluate your approach to the conversation.

Ideally, your boss's legs should be uncrossed and facing you. If your boss's legs are not facing you, you can use their placement to determine a thing or two about your boss's intentions. Look at the direction that your boss's legs are pointing. They may be pointing toward the door. This signifies that your boss may have someplace to go and would rather be there than meeting with you. If his or her legs are pointing toward the inside of his or her office, it may mean his or her mind is on work, and he or she would like to get back to it soon.

What if you do not like what you see?

Paying attention to your boss's body language will let you know whether your boss likes what you are saying or not. It is possible that you will see negative body language during your conversation with your boss. If this happens, do not panic. There is still time to sway your boss toward your side of the conversation.

Redirect the body

Remember that when it comes to body language, the brain can be directing the body, or the body's movement can direct the brain. So if you see your boss displaying negative body language, it is in your interest to get their body position to change as quickly as possible. Using subtle moves, you may be able to get your boss to change position and, in turn, change his or her mind about what you are saying, or at least make him or her more open to hearing more options.

The easiest way to redirect your boss's body language is to give your boss something to do with his or her hands. Hand him or her a copy of part of your presentation. Or put part of your presentation between the two of you and invite your boss to look at it with you. This will pull your boss's focus into your work and force him or her to change his or her body movement to accommodate looking at the presentation.

Change your own body language

If you are getting negative or resistant body language from your boss, it is possible that your boss is mirroring you. So you should check in with your own body language. Are your arms open and relaxed, or are they tight against your body? Are you smiling genuinely, or do you have a false smile on your face? Are you using your hands expressively, or do you have them tightly folded in your lap? Take a minute to relax and readjust your own body language to positively influence your boss.

Any adjustments you make in your body language should look organic and natural. Relax and move naturally. If you jerk into a new position, you will draw attention to your random movement more than you will influence your boss to think more positively about you.

Move to incorporate positive body language. Open your hands, relax your arms, and smile naturally. Sit forward in your chair to show you are excited about what you are saying. Widen your eyes a little. Even thinking of a happy memory while you are talking will cause your pupils to dilate and have a positive effect on your meeting with your boss.

Ask Questions

You will have much to say during your meeting with your boss about your raise. However, do not forget that your boss will have important things to say as well. If you are seeing negative body language from your boss, it may be possible that your boss wants to express some of those things and is not getting the chance to say them. Asking questions is a good way to open this door and allow your boss to speak.

Ask open-ended questions that will give your boss an opportunity to say more than a yes or a no. For example: "What do you think about that?" or "How does that sound?" These types of questions give your boss a chance to interact and can help alleviate any tension that may be causing your boss's negative body language.

Keep your defenses down

If, after employing positive countermeasures to any negative body language from your boss, you are still seeing resistant physical positioning, do not panic. There are a number of reasons that your boss could be upset or distracted. Ideally, your boss will give you his or her full attention. This is an important matter that you are discussing, after all. But if he or she does not, it may have nothing to do with you. So keep your guard down. Do not get defensive. Just continue the meeting being as personable and professional as you can. You may just win your boss over with your good attitude, in spite of his or her defensive one.

CHAPTER 13

Put It in Writing

In addition to your verbal presentation, you will also need to bring documentation to your meeting. You should have two copies of everything that you plan to discuss. One copy will be for you to refer to, and the other will be for your boss. You can leave the material with your boss when the meeting is over so he or she may refer to it while the final decision is being made.

Your presentation should consist of a cover letter and all your supporting material. The cover letter should be first, and the supporting material should follow in a logical order. The material should be free from spelling and grammar errors. Also, if you have photocopied or printed documents, these documents should be easy to read and free from stray lint or dust marks that may have been on the copier or printer. Having your material in a neat, easy-to-read presentation will make it simple for your boss to see that you have done your work, you are a solid communicator, and you are ready to receive a raise.

The Cover Letter

Writing a good cover letter is nearly an art form itself. A good cover letter should be informative and engaging. It should let the reader know exactly what you are hoping to get from him or her — or what you have to offer him or her. It should also show a bit of your personality and not get bogged down with formality.

Cover letters should follow business letter format. In the heading, you should use your home address for the return address and your boss's address at the company for the send-to address. The rest of the letter should follow standard business format. This will make your letter easy to read, and it will give your boss all the background information that he or she needs to understand what else is to come in your presentation.

The cover letter should also follow the style guidelines for writing a business letter. The opening paragraph should let your boss know you are looking for a raise. The following paragraphs should each offer support for and summarize the reasons why you deserve a raise. The final paragraph should list the specifics of what you are looking and should thank your boss for his or her time or consideration.

Follow the procedure discussed earlier to make sure your cover letter is free from errors. Print it out and read it somewhere other than on your computer screen. Run a spelling and grammar check. Read it out loud and see how it sounds to your ears. Your letter should sound friendly, professional, and persuasive.

Each supporting paragraph should summarize the major points of your presentation. You do not need to list every detail of your presentation for two reasons: First, you will be discussing each reason in detail; and second, your supporting material will also discuss your reasons for deserving a raise. Your supporting paragraphs should read something like this:

> My customer service record has been excellent. Last quarter, I successfully managed requests from high-end clients and not only met deadlines, but finished work well-ahead of those deadlines. One client was so happy with the work I performed that I received a wonderful thank-you letter the next day. In addition to this work, I also helped our team develop a method for streamlining e-mail returns. This allowed us to answer requests 25 percent faster than the previous quarter. Our customers have been happy with our service, and it has made me feel great to offer this service to them.

Follow this pattern in your cover letter for explaining your major points. This will keep your reasons organized in your boss's mind. It will also give your boss a teaser for what is to come in your presentation. Word your letter the right way, and your boss will likely be excited to see what else you have in store.

Remember not to read your letter to your boss when you sit down for your meeting. The letter is for your boss to reference after you have gone. Your boss may also show your letter to anyone he or she has to report to — another reason to make sure your letter is strong and error-free. This will not only get your boss's attention, but also the attention of anyone else who might read your letter.

Review career guides to get some additional advice about how to craft your cover letter. Many books and Web sites provide examples of completed cover letters. Do not copy these letters, but review their voice, style, and persuasive quality. See whether you can incorporate these elements into your own cover letter.

Cover letter dos and don'ts

Do:

- **Write an engaging letter.** Between new hires and other employees asking for raises, your boss has probably read countless cover letters. Make yours stand out by writing creatively. This does not mean straying from the subject, but try to give your letter a personal tone. Let your personality shine through. Your boss will not just be rewarding a raise to someone who can complete certain tasks, but to someone with whom he or she will likely have a relationship with for some time to come. Make your letter reflect the fact that you are a person who is interesting to know.

- **Check grammar, spelling, and punctuation.** A well-written letter is not only full of your wonderful personality, but also free from mistakes or errors. If you are using business terms, make sure you use them correctly. Big, complicated words are not always better, especially if they clutter up your letter or cause you to make usage mistakes. Keep it simple, and double-check your spell-check program.

- **Fact check.** If you are relying on any sort of statistical information, make sure it is correct. If you decide to reference specific information regarding your company, make sure you have your facts right before committing them to paper. Using incorrect facts may make it look as though you are trying to inflate your case, or that your case does not speak strongly enough for itself. Stick to the facts, and make sure you have everything in order.

- **Keep your letter on message.** Make sure you clearly state what your intentions are in the first paragraph, and that each paragraph after that supports your case. This is not the time to bring in everything that you have done since you started working. If a statement or sentiment does not point directly toward why you should receive a raise, save it for another presentation. Keeping your cover letter on-message will ensure your employer should be interested in reading it until the end and will put you closer to getting your raise.

- **Make it look nice.** In addition to having plenty of support explaining why you deserve a raise, your cover letter should look like something that an up-and-coming professional put together.

- **The font should be easy to read, and the letter itself should be centered on the page.** If possible, avoid "widows" or "orphans" in your paragraphs. These are lines of text that consist of one or two words. Try to write so that all lines of your paragraph extend more than half way across the centerline. It may be necessary to add or delete words for this to happen. Writing so your lines extend at least almost all the way across the page will make your letter look nicer and will help the eye flow naturally across the page.

- **Even your signature should look nice.** Practice signing your signature so that it is at least somewhat legible. It does not need to be perfect, printed script, but it should be readable and fit pleasingly between the closing and your typed name at the bottom of your cover letter.

However, the following should be avoided. Do not:

- **Be afraid to ask for what you want.** Do not assume you can avoid telling your employer that you want a raise. You must state clearly what your objectives are so that the rest of the letter makes sense. Do not be embarrassed about why you are here; many employees want raises. You should feel proud that you are confident enough in your abilities to ask for what you want. Unless you have slacked off and not done the preparation work, there is no reason why you should not feel confident asking for a raise. Make sure your cover letter clearly states what you are hoping for in this meeting.

- **Simply list what follows in your presentation.** Your cover letter should tie all the material together and draw a logical conclusion. If you have done your work properly, that conclusion is that you deserve a raise. Do not double up your work by restating what supporting documents you have brought with you to your meeting. Your employer will be able to see exactly what is in your presentation. If you do not offer him or her anything new in the cover letter, the supporting materials may seem more boring than persuasive.

- **Insult your boss by not addressing the cover letter to him or her.** Even though you may also end up talking to other executives or managers about your potential raise, you should address your cover letter to the person with whom you are meeting. Do not use a generic "Dear Sirs," "To Whom it May Concern," or "Dear Sir or Madam." You will be sitting across from this person, so there is no reason not to address it directly to him or her. If possible, address and personalize separate copies of your presentation to any other executives who may review it as well.

- **Write too much.** You want your meeting to be taken up with your scintillating conversation and compelling verbal arguments, not with your boss poring over a small novel you have placed on his or her desk. Do not add your own manifesto to your boss's reading list. Keep your cover letter short, concise, and to the point. The rest of the supporting material, and your presentation, will do most of the work for you. The cover letter is an important part, but remember that it is not the only part.

- **Use passive language.** Be assertive when you speak in your cover letter. Do not state issues in terms of your "feelings" or "thoughts." Rather, state them as facts. For example, avoid saying, "I think that you can see that my new filing system increased productivity." Instead, say confidently, "My new filing system increased productivity." It is the same set of facts, but the second sentence is not diluted by the subjectivity of your own thoughts.

Supporting Documents

Now is the time to organize all the written material you have collected as you have prepared for your raise. These materials may include:

- Recommendation letters or letters of praise from clients or supervisors
- Awards or recognition from the company
- Information on current salaries for your position
- Documentation of changes you have implemented
- Personal letters of recommendation from peers
- Awards or recognition from business-related organizations or clubs

Whatever documents you have, make sure they are easy to read and understand. Something like a recommendation letter, for example, will likely be self-explanatory. The letter will explain who is writing the letter and why they are writing it. If you have included a list or chart of salary information, you will need to clearly label the chart so anyone reading it will be able to easily understand what this information is. You do not want your boss to be confused by what he or she is looking at. If your boss cannot immediately grasp the information presented, your communication skills will be called into question, and your boss may be less likely to give you your raise.

To make sure you have collected all the supporting documents you can, consult the daily journal that was discussed in Chapter 4. Read through your entries and see whether you can find anything that would be helpful. Your journal should not be used as a supporting document; it should merely point you toward material that could be helpful to your case.

Keep it Brief

Your boss's time is precious, and so is yours. Be kind to both of you during your meeting and respect your time. Do not let your meeting drag on for too long. A succinct meeting should last between 20 and 30 minutes; the shorter and more efficient the better. You do not want to cut yourself short and leave out important information. However, you do not need to go over every point. You have a variety of supporting material ready, so all you need to do is give the highlights and let your supporting material do the rest of the talking.

To manage time, you need to be aware of the time. If your boss has a clock in his or her office, find ways to keep your eyes on it. Do not stare too long — you want to maintain eye contact with your boss, and too much looking around the room can look shifty, nervous, or suspicious. But if you can steal a glance now and then, do so. Likewise, if you have a watch, find quick ways of looking down and referencing it.

You can also time yourself with practice. Spend time going over your presentation at home or for peers. When you do, time yourself to see how long it takes. Try to get your presentation to be between 20 and 30 minutes. Even with added conversation or questions your boss may have, you can feel confident that your rehearsed presentation will fall within a reasonable time parameter.

Another way to control how long or short your meeting runs is through how you answer your boss's questions. Your answers should be short and to the point. You do not need to elaborate excessively when your boss asks you a question.

No Ultimatums or Demands

Though, ideally, you will be doing a good portion of the talking, your meeting about your raise needs to be a discussion. During the course of your presentation, you should allow time for both you and your boss to state your opinions, thoughts, ideas, and concerns. Avoid thinking of this meeting as a "you against them" situation. You want your employer to want to work with you, not to feel like you are standing up against them. So avoid making ultimatums or demands during your meeting.

You should not enter the meeting with the attitude that you are going to walk out if you do not get what you want. Although leaving your company to pursue stronger alternatives may be a viable option, you should not hold that over your boss's head. Upsetting the powers that be is rarely a good idea. And since your boss is ultimately in the power position, if you try to play a power game, you will probably lose.

Ask for what you want, but do not be demanding about it. It is perfectly reasonable to expect your boss to listen to what you have to say, but avoid being defensive if you do not immediately get the response you want. Keeping a cool head and addressing your boss with respect will win you more points than being demanding.

Be Honest

You may be tempted to inflate the work you have done to bolster your case. It is possible that your boss may not know about every little thing that goes on during his or her watch, or that he or she will not have the time to double-check every fact presented in your presentation. But as tempted as you may feel to fudge the facts, do not give in to that temptation.

Being less than honest in your presentation will only hurt you in the end. It may be that your boss does find out that you have been dishonest, and your job — not just your raise — may be on the line. It may be that you get yourself into a situation where your boss now expects more from you than you are able to give. Or it may be that you will constantly be looking over your shoulder to make sure no one is catching you in your mistruth.

If you have done the work described in this book, you will have little to worry about when it comes to finding ways to talk yourself up. You may not have completely retooled the company, but you will have put yourself on the path toward a stellar work record. Even small things can carry huge amounts of weight. Showing you are willing to stay late and arrive early; presenting yourself as a well-put-together professional; and speaking and writing effectively — all of these traits add up to one excellent worker and will provide the foundation for you to prove that you are worthy of additional compensation. An employee who has these attributes under his or her belt does not need to lie to make himself or herself look good.

Practice

By this time, you have done considerable work to get ready for your raise. Do not let performance-day jitters get in the way of what you have been working toward. Spend time before your meeting practicing your presentation. Go over each point of your presentation for time, clarity, and persuasiveness. Ask peers to review your presentation. Show it to them as you would to your boss. It would be best, however, to avoid showing your presentation to peers at the office. Instead, practice with other working professionals to get their opinion. Take your presentation to a trusted mentor in a higher position so that you can get the advice of someone closer to the level of your boss. If your presentation impresses them, you know that you will have a better chance of also impressing your boss.

Common Objections and How to Handle Them

You should be ready to handle objections should they arise. Even with a persuasive presentation that was delivered flawlessly, your boss may find reasons to hold back on your raise. Being able to effectively address this final roadblock to your raise may result in the paycheck you were hoping for.

The following are some common objections you may hear from your employer. He or she may phrase them differently, but listen to what they are saying and see if you can hear one of these themes coming through. You certainly want to respect anything your boss has to say about the potential for giving you a raise; however, you also want to be able to defend your position in an intelligent way.

Countering their objection with the right argument may put you back on the track to getting what you what you are looking for.

Remember to state your objections to their objections with respect and professionalism. This is not the time to get into a shouting match about who is right. Ultimately, your employer has the power in this situation, so you will want to respect that and make sure you state your own arguments with respect. Being able to successful handle objections is part of the job of any good business person. If you can successfully argue for your raise in spite of your employer's objections, you will make your raise more likely.

"We do not have the money"

If your boss indicates that there is simply not enough money coming into the company to give anyone anymore, you will have to be clever to avoid simply walking away at this point. You do not want to imply that you think that there is more money than your boss is letting on; you do not want to push your boss to do something financially risky for the company; and you do not want to simply fold and walk away.

One way to get around this objection is to plan for the future. Let your boss know you understand that money may be tight, but that you have faith that the company will see stronger profits in the future. And when that happens, you would like to incorporate your raise into those profits.

Another way to handle this objection is to lean more heavily on non-pay benefits, as were discussed earlier. Many of these benefits, such as profit sharing and stock option plans, are tied into how much the company is making. Other types of benefits, including a shorter workweek or additional vacation time, may also be a good alternative until business picks up again.

If low company profits are getting in the way of your raise, you should plan to revisit the issue with your boss at a later time. Take care to stay on top of company information. When business picks up again, remember to schedule time with your boss to discuss your raise again.

"You already make more than others here"

It is possible that you are at the high end of your pay range. You may already be making more than your peers in the office. While this may be true, it does not mean you are not entitled to more. Your pay rate should be based on your job performance and industry standards, and should not have much to do with anyone else in the office.

This is where all your research comes into play. If you have found your company tends to pay less than other similar companies in the area, you can use that information in a strong way against this argument. You should encourage your boss to look at your salary in terms of the industry, not just his or her own office.

If your boss does mention the salaries of others in the office, let him or her know you have not been snooping through employee records to find out what others make. Then shift the focus back to you and your work. Saying something like, "Well, I am not aware of what my coworkers are earning each year, but I know that my work record in the last three quarters shows that I have contributed significantly to the bottom line." A statement like this puts the focus back where it should be during this discussion — on you. This meeting is not about anyone except you. Do what you can to keep it that way.

"It is not up to me"

It may be that the person you report to has someone he or she reports to who will need to sign off on your raise. In large companies, this is certainly to be expected. But this is another instance where your planning and organization will help you in your presentation.

Your boss probably has many other issues to attend to, so taking a persuasive conversation to his or her boss on behalf of someone else may not be at the top of his or her list. However, if your presentation is well-organized, you have done most of the work for your boss.

If your boss gives you this objection, show him or her how simple, clear, and effective your presentation is. Quickly review the main points and point them out in your physical presentation. Offer to simplify it even further if that would make things easier. It might be that you can sit in on the meeting with the person your boss reports to and thus take the burden of explanation off of your boss's shoulders. Offer this as a solution as well.

Additionally, if you have done your research properly, you may already know a thing or two about the person your boss reports to. Maybe you have found out that executive is more concerned with cultivating a team approach than he or she is about individual performance. You can mention information like this to your boss with a statement like, "I know you will need to speak to Mr. Rodriguez about my potential raise. I also know that he is excited to see more teambuilding it the departments. I think you will find that my team approach to the Thompson case will be something Mr. Rodriguez will definitely be interested in hearing about."

Final advice on objections

While it may be frustrating to hear objections to your well-researched presentation, do not take objections personally. Some initial resistance may have nothing to do with you. Your employer is dealing with the entire company, not just you. Expect many factors of which you are not aware to affect your boss's response to your presentation.

The best thing you can do is to be prepared, calm, and respectful. Your boss will appreciate a concise, persuasive presentation. You will make yourself into a more valuable asset for your company if you keep your attitude in check instead of getting defensive if and you encounter resistance.

To Review

This is the big moment. All your hard work has been leading up to this presentation. Carefully review the information and key points to make sure your meeting is as effective as possible.

- **Make an appointment**. It may sound like it goes without saying, but make sure you get your raise discussion meeting down in the books. Be flexible with your meeting time, and make sure the meeting accommodates both your and your boss's schedule.

- **This is your meeting.** Control it. You have set this meeting for a specific purpose, and you have a specific goal. Resist the urge to lighten the mood by discussing other issues. Be friendly, but make sure you get your points out and your presentation completed.

- **Stay confident.** You have done considerable work to get to this point. You should feel confident about the good work you have done. The confidence you project toward your boss will only strengthen your case.

- **Respect your relationship.** If you and your boss have a formal, distant relationship, do not use this time to try and become his or her best friend. If you are too chummy instead of respecting the boundaries that exist between the two of you, you will weaken your case. Be professional and adhere to the natural distance or closeness in your relationship.

- **Do not overstay your welcome.** Your meeting should not be longer than about 20 minutes. Your boss is probably busy, and with all the work you have been doing to prove yourself, you are too. Respect everyone's time and keep the meeting brief.

- **Use language effectively.** Leading statements and questions will help bring your boss into your conversation. Asking yes or no questions will not facilitate discussion, and you want your boss to be involved in this talk.

- **Body language.** Plenty of information is exchanged without any words at all. Make sure your body language is inviting and warm. Using positive body language can even help you feel more confident.

- **Contagious nodding.** Nod slightly when you want to illicit a positive response or when describing something positive. People tend to imitate body language as well as the feelings that go with them. Nodding while you speak may lead your boss to be more agreeable with what you are saying.

- **Keep your hands open and expressive.** Folding your hands and keeping them still may appear off-putting and aggressive. You should also avoid pointing while you speak.

- **Copy what your boss is doing.** As you start your meeting, take care to notice how your boss is sitting, and mirror their stance. Mirroring happens naturally between friends and relatives. Mirroring your boss on purpose may illicit additional agreement in your presentation. Mirroring his or her mannerisms with your speech pattern is another way to foster agreement and friendly feelings.

- **Smile.** People like to see positive faces looking back at them. Smiles are disarming and create positive feelings.

- **Avoid clenching your fists, crossing your arms over your body, picking at your clothes, or covering your mouth with your hands.** These motions can be seen as aggressive or insincere.

- **Take care to read your boss's body language.** Doing so will help you know whether you are being effective. If you see negative body language, you should adjust your approach — and your own body language — to illicit a more positive response.

- **Using effective body language is a skill, like good writing or speaking well.** You will need to practice. Watch your body language in a mirror before your presentation so that you can use it effectively.

- **Write everything down.** Remember to bring your physical presentation with you. You should have your documentation, cover letter, and other supporting materials assembled in an easy-to-navigate packet.

- **Remember that you are making a case, not laying down the law.** You should avoid threatening or making ultimatums. You want to engage your boss in a conversation, and not a heated debate.

- **Be honest.** Do not over-inflate your accomplishments or your intentions. Your meeting should serve as an accurate review of what you have done and what you intend to do with your new pay rate.

- **Rehearse your presentation.** Know your lines and be ready to go when it is show time.

- **Be ready to handle common objections.** Keep your cool but speak to your case.

End High

Regardless of the immediate outcome, you should strive to end your meeting on a positive note. If it is clear that you may not get your raise at this time, try shifting the focus of the conversation to a more positive topic. Ask your boss for advice on a project, or congratulate him or her on a recent success. When you excuse yourself, let your boss know that you are headed back to your desk, office, or cubicle to get right back to work. Do not give the impression that you are about to relax for a minute or blow off some steam.

If it looks like your raise is a sure thing, be professional and restrained with your reaction. Ask for clarification on any of the details you may be wondering about — when the raise will go into effect, whether there is any paperwork you need to fill out, or whether there is another department you should schedule time with to work out the final details. Regardless of what happens, thank your boss for the time he or she spent with you in your meeting. Ask for advice on how you could have done things better or on how your boss thinks you should handle the next step. Reiterate the common goals that you discussed in the meeting. Leave the office with a smile and a handshake.

The end of the meeting is one last chance to cement a positive decision or change a negative one. If you leave the meeting with a clear answer on your raise, leaving positively may be the final push your boss needs to go ahead and sign off on the check. Conversely, if you leave visibly frustrated, angry, or ruffled, that may be all your boss needs to assume that you do not deserve that raise after all.

CHAPTER 14

Keep Going

Congratulations! Most of the work is now behind you. But do not slack off just because the meeting is over. What you do in the days and weeks following your raise request can still affect your raise. Following are ways to make sure you get — and keep — your raise.

CASE STUDY: MARIANNE HARTGRAVES

Marianne Hartgraves
Franchising manager
Parrottsville, Tennessee

Marianne Hartgraves served as franchising manager for McDonald's Corp. on the East Coast but is now retired. She explained the obstacles that prevent a supervisor from giving an employee a pay raise:

CASE STUDY: MARIANNE HARTGRAVES

"Lack of power to give raises, no money available, a supervisor who plays favorites, a supervisor who is poorly paid herself and does not want people in his or her department to make more than he or she does, and a supervisor who is not aware of what her employees have accomplished so is hesitant to give raises can be the obstacles that prevent a supervisor from giving pay raises."

Hartgraves said there are several actions employees should not do when requesting a pay raise: Do not complain about fellow workers, the job, or that you are underpaid. Do not threaten to leave if you do not get the raise or promotion. If you do not get a raise and you are unhappy, keep your own counsel and start looking for something else, she added.

Also, according to Hartgraves, never advertise that you are looking for another position to scare your supervisor into giving you a raise. It rarely works. Do not discuss politics, religion, or current controversial issues in the news, and do not talk about your family or your children. Never go for the pity raise, e.g., "I have four mouths to feed, my credit card payment is overdue, my car is broken down," because the supervisor does not care, and you are wasting time.

Hartgraves emphasizes focusing on your job and what you can offer your employer to make you more valuable to them. If your supervisor starts complaining to you, do not sympathize, empathize, or add your own tidbits. Try to get the conversation back on track. They will always remember what you said and probably repeat it to someone else. Remember: All the employer thinks of is, "What is in it for me or my company?"

Document

After your meeting, send a thank-you e-mail to your boss. This e-mail will serve three purposes. First, a thank-you note is a professional, polite gesture that will remind your boss you are someone with whom he or she would like to continue to work. Second, it will give you the chance to remind your boss of any high points of the meeting, and it will ensure the two of you remember the meeting similarly. And finally, it will provide a paper trail so that evidence of the meeting can be found.

Your e-mail may read something like this:

> Dear Mr. Romero,
>
> Thank you very much for meeting with me about my raise today. I appreciate your taking the time, and I look forward to using your advice as I finish the marketing reports this week. The streamlined system I developed for filing these reports is an example of the kind of work I look forward to doing with Our Company in the future.

It is important to keep a paper trail about your meeting for a few reasons. If your boss says he or she will give you an answer about your raise within a certain time period, the e-mail will provide a definite date on which the meeting occurred. This will allow you to check back in and get your answer in the time promised. Also, your human resources department will want to know about your meeting in case they need to reference it in the future. Finally, whether you stay at the company for the rest of your career or eventually leave it, you will want to have a record of as much that happened as possible.

Keep Up the Momentum

Now that you have stepped up your game, keep riding that high. If you immediately go back to old, less professional work habits, you will dilute all your hard work. It is possible that your boss will need a little while to consider your raise, or he or she may have other management-level employees to take your raise presentation to. If you immediately slack off, you will not be showing that you have the follow-through to be trusted with your raise. The extra effort you have put into getting your raise will look like a ploy and not like the genuine work ethic of a person whom your company will want to reward. But keep your skills, motivation, and drive high, and you will be well on your way to professional success — and many raises to come.

Bibliography

"52 Proven Stress Reducers," **www.twu.edu/o-sl/counseling/ SelfHelp001.html**, 2007.

Asher, Donald, *Who Gets Promoted and Who Doesn't and Why*, Ten Speed Press, Berkeley, California, 2007.

Batiz-Romero, Jenaro, Media Relations Manager, Personal Interview, May 19, 2008.

Batts, Gregory, "How to Get the Raise You Deserve," **www.ask-men.com**, IGN Entertainment, 1996-2008.

Bell, Brad, Entertainment Entrepreneur, Personal Interview, May 20, 2008.

Breus, Michael, PhD, ABSM, "How Much Sleep Do You Really Need?" **https://www.webmd.com**, 2004.

Brinkman, Steve, "The 8 Building Blocks of a Good Business Wardrobe," **http://suityourselfclothing.blogspot.com/2009/05 /8-building-blocks-of-good-business.html**.

"Career Exploration," **www.careerinfonet.org/EXPLORE/view. aspx?pageID=3**.

Cudd, Alonza, Marketing Consultant, Personal Interview, April 29, 2008.

"Employee Compensation," **www.referenceforbusiness.com/ management/Em-Exp/Employee-Compensation.html**, Advameg, Inc., 2007.

Franzinger, Kathleen. "Year in review: Annual performance reviews may vex managers and employees alike, but they can serve as useful communication tools." *Machine Design*, August 22, 2002.

Goldberg, Joan Rachel, "Helping Yourself to a Good Night's Sleep," National Sleep Foundation, 2007.

Hansen, Katherine and Randall, Ph.Ds, "Cover Letter Do's and Don'ts," **www.quintcareers.com/cover_letter-dos-donts.html**.

Hansen, Katharine and Randall, Ph.Ds, "The Dynamic Cover Letter Formula for Job-Search Success," **www.quintcareers. com/cover_letters.html**.

Karseras, Hugh, *From New Recruit to High Flyer*, Kogan Page Limited, London, 2006.

Krannich, Ron and Caryl, Ph.Ds, "Get a Raise in 7 Days, Impact Publications," Manassas Park, Virginia, 1999.

McEnroe, Meg, Office Manager, Personal Interview, May 24, 2008

Neal, Annie, Account Executive, Personal Interview, April 15, 2008.

Paskin, Janet. "How to Kick the High Cost of Child Care." Money 35.5, May 2006.

Pease, Allan and Barbara, *The Definitive Book of Body Language*, Bantam Dell, New York, 2004.

Post, Anna, Author and Spokesperson, Emily Post Institute, Personal Interview, April 23, 2008.

Reinhold, Barbara B., Ed.D, "Back to School: Returning for Your Degree," **www.collegeinfo.com/returning-to-school**.

Rich, Jason R., *Get That Raise*, Entrepreneur Media, Inc., Canada, 2007.

Russell, Francine, Personal Interview, April 20, 2008.

Ryan, Liz, "How to Get a Raise," *Business Week*, April 26, 2007.

Saether, Linda, "Water is Vital, but How Much Should You Drink?" **www.cnn.com/2008/HEALTH/05/16/hfh.water. guidelines/index.html**.

Speisman, Stephanie, "10 Tips for Successful Business Networking," **http://businessknowhow.com/tips/networking.htm**, Altard Communications, 1999-2008.

Stead, Mark, "12 Tips for an Organized Desk," **www.productivity501.com/12-tips-for-an-organized-desk/151/**, 2007.

"Study: expensive child care costs are 'parent trap' for families." Report on Preschool Programs 38.3, Feb 8, 2006, 22.

Thomas, Brandon, Owner Azarra Entertainment, Personal Interview, May 20, 2008.

Tracy, Brian, *Get Paid More and Promoted Faster, 21 Great Ways to Get Ahead in Your Career*, Berrett-Koehler Publishers, Inc., San Francisco, 2001.

U.S. Department of Labor, Employment Standards Administration Wage and Hour Division, **www.dol.gov/esa/whd/about/ whdabout.htm**.

Villanova, Peter Ph.D., Professor Appalachian State University, Personal Interview, May 1, 2008.

Walden, Kathy, Personal Interview, May 15, 2008.

Wong, Dan, "Thirteen Networking Mistakes," **http://career-advice.monster.com**.

Zamora, Dulce, "Sleep Deprivation at the Workplace," **www.webmd.com/sleep-disorders/guide/sleep-deprivation-workplace**.

Zupek, Rachel, "What Not to do When Asking for a Raise," **www.cnn.com/2007/LIVING/worklife/12/07/cb.get.a.raise/index.html**.